The More Effective Use of Resources

AN IMPERATIVE FOR HIGHER EDUCATION

A Report and Recommendations by

The Carnegie Commission on Higher Education

JUNE 1972

MCGRAW-HILL BOOK COMPANY

New York   St. Louis   San Francisco   Düsseldorf

London   Sydney   Toronto   Mexico   Panama

Johannesburg   Kuala Lumpur   Montreal

New Delhi   Rio de Janeiro   Singapore

This report is issued by the Carnegie Commission on
Higher Education, with headquarters at
1947 Center Street, Berkeley, California 94704.
The views and conclusions expressed in this report
are solely those of the members of the Carnegie Commission
on Higher Education and do not necessarily reflect the
views or opinions of the Carnegie Corporation of New York,
The Carnegie Foundation for the Advancement of Teaching,
or their trustees, officers, directors, or employees.

Library of Congress Cataloging in Publication Data

Carnegie Commission on Higher Education.
The more effective use of resources.

Includes bibliographical references.
1. Universities and colleges—Administration.
2. Universities and colleges—Finance.   3.   Education,
Higher—Costs.   I.   Title.
LB2341.C165   378.73   72-4368
ISBN 0-07-010051-9

Additional copies of this report may be ordered from
McGraw-Hill Book Company, Hightstown, New Jersey 08520.
The price is $3.95 a copy.

Ever higher costs [are] an inevitable characteristic of live performance.

WILLIAM BAUMOL AND WILLIAM BOWEN

Performing Arts: The Economic Dilemma

Contents

Foreword, vii

1 *Major Themes,* 1

2 *Dimensions of the Financial Crisis,* 27

3 *The Behavior of Costs,* 33

4 *Acceleration and Integration of Programs,* 49

5 *Retention Rates and the "Captive Audience,"* 59

6 *Utilization of Faculty Time,* 63

1. Student-faculty ratios ▪ 2. The size of classes ▪ 3. The proliferation of courses ▪ 4. Teaching loads ▪ 5. Research and public service ▪ 6. Consulting activities ▪ 7. Leaves of absence ▪ 8. Support personnel ▪ 9. A summing up

7 *Faculty Salaries and the Possible Impacts of Unionization,* 87

8 *Achieving Budgetary Flexibility,* 91

Selective cutbacks ▪ Across-the-board cuts ▪ Consolidating existing programs ▪ Readapting certain programs ▪ Every tub on its own bottom ▪ Reallocation of vacated positions

9 *Incentives for Constructive Change and Innovation,* 107

10 *Special Problems of a Period of Declining Rate of Growth,* 111

11 *The Planning and Control of Capital Costs,* 119

12 *Other Avenues to Effective Use of Resources,* 127

1. Consortia and interinstitutional cooperation ▪ 2. Management development ▪ 3. Administrative costs ▪ 4. Computer costs ▪ 5. Overcoming medical and dental school deficits ▪ 6. Auxiliary enterprises ▪ 7. Student aid policies ▪ 8. Financing student services

13 *The Management of Income and Endowment,* 143

1. Tuition policy ▪ 2. Effective student recruitment ▪ 3. Cash balances and inventories ▪ 4. Managing endowment funds

14 *Concluding Note,* 151

Appendix A: Statistical Tables, 153

Appendix B: Note on PPBS and Institutional Research in Higher Education, 159

Appendix C: Economies of Scale, 163

Appendix D: Excerpt from Statement on Faculty Workload of the American Association of University Professors, 191

Introduction ▪ Maximum teaching loads ▪ Procedures

References, 195

Foreword

During the years since World War II, higher education in the United States has experienced extraordinary growth. It is now serving nearly 7 million more students than were enrolled in the early postwar years, and many of these are low-income and minority-group students for whom financial and other barriers to entry into higher education have been substantially lowered. Although we still have a long way to go before we achieve complete equality of opportunity in higher education, the progress made in the last decade has been impressive.

The postwar research achievements of American higher education also have been impressive. The quality of scientific research in our universities is now regarded as the highest in the world and has created the basis for many breakthroughs in combatting disease and in the conquest of space. Looking to the coming decades, there is growing appreciation of the need for equally vigorous research efforts directed toward the solution of urban problems and the protection of the environment.

However, the confidence of higher education in its capacity to achieve continued progress toward equality of opportunity and toward the advancement of knowledge has been shaken in the last few years by the development of an unprecedented financial crisis. This financial crisis results, in part, from the extraordinary rapidity of the rate of growth in the 1950s and 1960s, and the heavy increases in expenditures that accompanied that growth. Not only were expenditures rising to accommodate the ever increasing number of students, but higher education was also assuming greatly expanded responsibilities for research and public service. This is one-half of the financial crisis.

For a variety of reasons—the war in Vietnam, the growing fiscal difficulties of the states, public resentment over student unrest and

student behavior, the recession that began at the end of 1969—
toward the end of the 1960s funds were not forthcoming in amounts
sufficient to maintain the rate of increase in total expenditures on
higher education that had characterized the earlier part of the
decade. This is the other half of the financial crisis.

One solution to the crisis is the more effective use of resources.
What do we mean by more effective use of resources within higher
education? Among other things we mean that an institution should
(1) carefully analyze the relations between the use of resources and
the accomplishment of goals, (2) seek maximum economies with
minimal sacrifices in quality, and (3) encourage rapid and flexible
adaptation to changes in needs for educational, research, and public
service programs.

We do not mean that expenses should be pruned regardless of the
effects of such pruning on quality or on the scope of service.
Economies can be achieved without sacrificing quality and many
of the measures discussed in this report, such as changes in degree
structures and elimination of overlapping and duplication of degree
programs, e.g., in the health sciences, would achieve more economical use of resources without sacrifices in the quality of education.

Although this report will be concerned primarily with more effective use of resources within institutions of higher education,
whether they be single-campus or multicampus institutions, efforts
of individual institutions to achieve more effective use of resources
will also contribute to more effective use of resources within society
as a whole, unless those economizing measures adopted by institutions simply shift burdens of expense to someone else. For
example, achieving more effective utilization of space and thus
holding down the need for more construction is an economy for the
institution and for society, but eliminating a subsidy from cafeteria
operations helps the institution to balance its budget while shifting
some costs to students. That does not mean that eliminating
subsidies from cafeteria operations may not be desirable, but it
does mean that we must be careful to distinguish between savings
for institutions and savings for society as a whole. We shall seek to
set forth the aggregative savings for institutions and for society
which we believe are reasonably possible.

In emphasizing the importance of effective use of resources, the
Commission does not mean to imply that the most significant functions of institutions of higher education are administrative functions. Colleges and universities are engaged in the transmission and

advancement of knowledge, in teaching their students how to tackle complex problems and issues so that the process of continued learning can proceed effectively throughout their lives, and in providing an environment in which students can resolve the conflicts in values and outlooks that tend to seem particularly important in the college-age years. And, increasingly in the future, colleges and universities will be providing an environment in which adults can participate in higher education. But if they are to accomplish these purposes effectively, they must make wise decisions about the allocation of their resources and the use of their highly educated faculties, and they must be prepared to achieve more rapid adaptation to changing needs than has generally been characteristic of higher education in the past.

The Commission has earlier recommended greater expenditures of federal and state and private funds on higher education. And it has always felt that it had an obligation to recommend how these new funds and existing funds could best be spent. Thus this report.

The Commission has sponsored several studies concerned with the fiscal situation of higher education, in particular: *Alternative Methods of Federal Funding for Higher Education,* by Ron Wolk (McGraw-Hill, 1969); *The Economics of the Major Private Universities,* by William G. Bowen (Carnegie Commission on Higher Education, Berkeley, 1968); *The Finance of Higher Education,* by Howard R. Bowen (Carnegie Commission on Higher Education, Berkeley, 1968); *Financing Medical Education: An Analysis of Alternative Policies and Mechanisms,* by Rashi Fein and Gerald I. Weber (McGraw-Hill, 1971); *The New Depression in Higher Education: A Study of Financial Conditions at 41 Colleges and Universities,* by Earl F. Cheit (McGraw-Hill, 1971); *Papers on Efficiency in the Management of Higher Education,* by Alexander Mood, Lawrence Bogard, Colin Bell, Helen Brownlee, and Joseph Mc-Closkey (Carnegie Commission on Higher Education, Berkeley, 1972); *A Statistical Portrait of Higher Education,* by Seymour E. Harris (McGraw-Hill, 1972); *Resource Use in Higher Education: Trends in Output and Inputs, 1930–1967,* by June O'Neill (Carnegie Commission on Higher Education, Berkeley, 1971).

To the many persons who were consulted and gave us helpful suggestions, we wish to express our appreciation. A particularly valuable contribution was made by Acting Provost Joseph Kershaw, Williams College.

The Commission has benefitted greatly from the advice of a

number of people and particularly the individuals who participated in conferences on the subject of this report at the invitation of the Commission. We express our appreciation to: Dr. Raymond F. Bacchetti, associate provost and director, Academic Planning Office, Stanford University; Dr. Sidney W. Brossman, chancellor, California Community Colleges; Dr. John Caffrey, president, Educational Systems Research Group; Dr. Allan Cartter, chancellor, New York University; Dr. Earl F. Cheit, program advisor, The Ford Foundation; E. Alden Dunham, executive associate, Carnegie Corporation of New York; Dr. Winfred Godwin, director, Southern Regional Education Board; Dr. Paul Grambsch, professor of management and director, Center for Academic Administration Research, University of Minnesota; Dr. Stanley J. Heywood, president, Eastern Montana College, and member, Carnegie Commission on Higher Education; William W. Jellema, research director, Association of American Colleges; Dr. Hans H. Jenny, vice president for finance and business, College of Wooster; Dr. Richard W. Judy, principal, Systems Research Group, University of Toronto; Dr. Charles V. Kidd, director, Council on Federal Relations, The Association of American Universities; Dr. Ben Lawrence, director, National Center for Higher Education Management Systems, Western Interstate Conference on Higher Education; Dr. William Lewis, director of analytical studies, Office of the Vice President—Planning and Analysis, University of California; Dr. Richard Peterson, research psychologist, Educational Testing Service; Dr. Roy Radner, professor of economics, University of California, Berkeley; Dr. George Weathersby, assistant director for analytical studies, Office of the Vice President—Planning and Analysis, University of California; Dr. John T. Wilson, provost, University of Chicago; and Dr. John M. Wynne, vice president for administration and personnel, Massachusetts Institute of Technology.

The Commission also expresses its debt to the members of its staff and especially to Dr. Margaret S. Gordon and David Datz.

Eric Ashby
The Master
Clare College
Cambridge, England

Ralph M. Besse
Chairman of the Board
National Machinery Company

The More Effective Use of Resources

1. Major Themes

1   Higher education in the United States has just completed its decade of greatest academic success. In the 1960s it more than doubled its enrollments (from over three million to over six million students on a full-time equivalent—FTE—basis) without a reduction in quality of instruction. It became the preeminent world center for research.

    Yet higher education in the early 1970s is experiencing its greatest financial crisis.

    This anomalous juxtaposition of triumph and depression is a fact that must be accepted, and adjustments must be made to it. It may seem unfair to some; it may be welcomed by others; but it remains a dominant reality in higher education and in American society.

2   The central thrust of this report is that the total institutional expenditures of higher education must be, should be, and can be reduced by nearly $10 billion per year (in 1970 dollars) by 1980 as compared with the costs which would be incurred if the trends of the 1960s were to be continued; that expenditures should be held to a level of around $41.5 billion as against $51 billion per year. This is approximately a 20-percent reduction. This would mean that these expenditures would rise to 2.7 percent of the GNP as compared with their present percentage of 2.5 and as compared with the possibility of 3.3 percent if the trends of the 1960s were to be continued and as against about 1.0 percent in the year 1960. We seek to show both why this reduction of about 20 percent needs to take place and how it can be accomplished without any general deterioration in the quality of higher education.

3   Why is there a crisis that calls for such a drastic adjustment in the 1970s as against the trends of the 1960s?

(1) The quantitative and qualitative growth of the 1960s raised total costs in several ways. The student body more than doubled. The output of high-cost Ph.D.'s tripled. The new student body required more remedial work and more student aid from institutional, as well as external, funds. New programs were added, for example, in ethnic studies and ecology. Computers were introduced on a large scale. The heavy capital investments also led to greatly increased costs for building maintenance. Many new research institutes and endeavors were added. And there were also some costs in terms of fast promotions and added amenities that resulted from 20 years of high demand for faculty members. Some institutions became overcommitted in the euphoria of growth; they tried to move up too far and too fast in the academic world in relation to their available resources. The number of institutions giving the Ph.D. degree, for example, increased from 180 to 250. Many campuses found it hard to slow their growth and slow their expectations as the period of rapid expansion ended. Even now, about 70 communities plan to start new medical schools when the nation requires only about 10 percent of this number; and about 150 colleges and universities plan to introduce Ph.D. programs for the first time[1] when no more at all are needed. The momentum is there and it is hard to slow it down.

(2) Beyond the momentum of growth was the inflation of costs per student. The rate of general inflation rose from about 2 percent at the beginning of the 1960s to 5 percent at the beginning of the 1970s. And inflation is always hard on colleges and universities (1, pp. 422–429). Furthermore, some costs important to higher education—for books, for construction, for faculty salaries—rose more than the average. Faculty salaries rose cumulatively about 1 percent faster per year than average earnings for all Americans (nearly 6 versus nearly 5 percent); and faculty salaries are one-third of all educational costs (aside from organized research). Faculty salaries, it should be realized, however, were historically low prior to the 1960s as compared with incomes in many other professions.

(3) Growth was up and cost per unit was up, but the increase in income leveled off. Higher education began to be ground between the upper and the nether millstones. The campuses bore the brunt of the great political controversies of the 1960s over the war in Viet Nam and over racial justice; and the resulting dissent and disruption disenchanted the public. Other great priorities came to national attention—renovation of cities, preservation of the environment, reduction of poverty, and many others. A recession slowed down the nation in general and state revenues in particular. "Stagflation" is a very poor environment for both the income and the costs of higher education. Also, higher education may be reaching a ceiling in the amount

---

[1] See Lewis B. Mayhew, *Graduate and Professional Education, 1980,* McGraw-Hill, New York, 1970, p. 2.

of money it can expect from society—it used about 1 percent of the GNP in 1960 and is using 2.5 percent now, and no other segment of society more than doubled its take of the GNP during that short period of time. A resistance point may have been reached.

For these three reasons a confrontation has developed between institutional expectations and the hard realities of the national situation. Collisions, little and big, are shaking the structure of higher education.

Chart 1 shows how current fund expenditure increases have been going down since 1968 while inflation has been reducing the net increases since 1966. New money has been coming in at a reduced rate and more of it has been taken up by inflation.

CHART 1 *Annual percent change in total current fund expenditures by institutions of higher education, and annual percent change in the consumer price index, fiscal years 1960 to 1971*

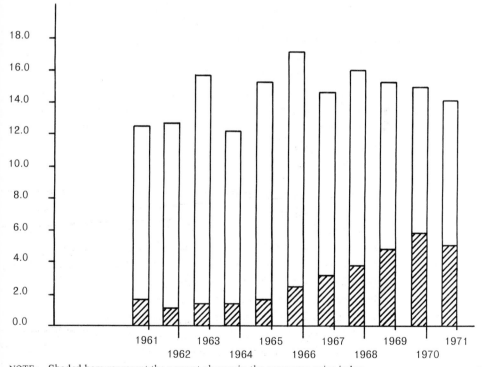

NOTE: Shaded bars represent the percent change in the consumer price index.

SOURCE: U.S. Office of Education, *Projections of Educational Statistics to 1979–80,* Washington, 1970, pp. 101–102; *Chronicle of Higher Education,* April 17, 1972, p. 1; *Economic Report of the President,* Washington, 1972, p. 247.

Different institutions have been affected differently. Generally, the private institutions have suffered the most—they had the highest average costs per student in 1960, and these costs rose the fastest over the decade. As extreme cases, elite institutions in ghetto areas suddenly called upon to serve the surrounding community, like the University of Chicago and Columbia University, were placed under great stress; also, some of the liberal arts colleges and the private junior colleges faced more intense competition from low-tuition public colleges. By contrast, the public community colleges have done well—they have had almost no student dissent, their operating costs are relatively low, they make the best night and Saturday use of their capital investment, they are close to their communities politically. Thus the private colleges have generally been the first to experience the cost-increase bind. How they meet it is of interest to all higher education, but many public institutions, particularly the public universities, have also been strongly affected.

Rather than a single financial crisis in higher education, there are many crises. Different institutions and different types of institutions have been affected to quite varied degrees, some fatally and some hardly at all. The major problems have come from different directions—here from a reduction in federal research support, there from a great increase in the student aid account, elsewhere from reduced state appropriations—but above and beyond each of the individual crises lies the general reduction in the rate of increase in real resources. Higher education, overall, is being put under more financial pressure.

4 At a minimum, higher education must get back to its historic (1930 to 1960) rate of increase in cost per student per year (or cost per student credit hour) of the general rate of inflation plus 2.5 percent; when, for example, the rate of general inflation has been 2.5 percent per year, the rate of increase in cost per unit for higher education has been 5 percent. This "plus 2.5 percent" has been necessary in order to offset the lack of productivity increases in higher education. Elsewhere in the economy, productivity has risen about 2.5 percent per year; while in higher education there has been no measurable productivity offset over the long-run (2) and costs have risen a plus 2.5 percent a year as wages and salaries on campus have kept up with the general rise in wages and salaries. To illustrate:

	Economy as a whole	Higher education
Rise in wages and salaries	5 %	5 %
Rise in productivity	2.5	0
Net rise in costs	2.5	5
Excess over the general rate of inflation	0	+2.5

Higher education, thus, is like the performing arts and other "service" sectors. Costs of the New York Philharmonic Orchestra rose a plus 3.5 percent a year (1920 to 1964) and of the Metropolitan Opera a plus 4 percent a year (1951 to 1964). Baumol and Bowen (3) explain these rises as follows:

The immediate result of this technological difference between live performance and the typical manufacturing industry is that while productivity is very much subject to change in the latter, it is relatively immutable in the former. Whereas the amount of labor necessary to produce a typical manufactured product has constantly declined since the beginning of the industrial revolution, it requires about as many minutes for Richard II to tell his "sad story of the death of kings" as it did on the stage of the Globe Theatre. Human ingenuity has devised ways to reduce the labor necessary to produce an automobile, but no one has yet succeeded in decreasing the human effort expended at a live performance of a 45-minute Schubert quartet much below a total of three man hours.

The same holds true for the "live performance" of teaching, research, and public service. Baumol and Bowen continue:

The central point of the argument is that for an activity such as the live performing arts where productivity is stationary, every increase in money wages will be translated automatically into an equivalent increase in unit labor costs — there is no offsetting increase in output per man-hour as there is in a rising productivity industry. This leads to an important corollary: the extent of the increase in relative costs in these activities where productivity is stationary will vary directly with the economy-wide rate of increase in output per man-hour. The faster the general pace of technological advance, the greater will be the increase in the over-all wage level, and the greater will be the upward pressure on costs in any industry which does not enjoy increased productivity.

An extreme case of a service industry with fast rising per-unit costs is health care. Hospital daily service charges rose at a plus 7.5 percent per year in the 1960s.

The plus 2.5 percent rise in cost per unit in higher education has been necessary for the reason given above. It has also been possible because the public has been willing to spend more of its income on higher education as income has risen—the demand is "income elastic." Even as the relative price of higher education has risen, as against goods and services generally, the public has both paid the price and increased the quantity demanded. The demand, thus, is like that for foreign travel or membership in private clubs; and the opposite of that for bread or potatoes where the percentage of income spent per capita as income rises declines almost regardless of what happens to their relative prices. Per capita disposable income has risen in real terms about 2.5 percent a year and this matches the rise in the price paid per unit for higher education; its price in general and its tuition in particular have been tied to the rise in disposable income. At the same time, the quantity demanded has also greatly increased. The higher price per unit and the greater quantity consumed taken together explain the rise in the percentage of the GNP going into higher education.

Thus the necessary plus 2.5 percent increase because of the negative productivity factor has been matched by the possible plus 2.5 percent increase because of the positive demand factor. Higher education has had to charge more and the public has been willing to pay it —and still ask for more in quantitative terms. The lag in the productivity increase has been offset by the income-elasticity of demand.

But many institutions went beyond the plus 2.5 percent per student per year to plus 4, or plus 5, or plus 6, or even plus 8 in the 1960s.[2]

The minimum imperative is to get back to a plus 2.5 percent level of increase on a continuing basis.

5 A harsher imperative may now be asserting itself—to get down below plus 2.5 percent per student per year:

---

[2] See Earl F. Cheit, *The New Depression in Higher Education*, McGraw-Hill, New York, 1971, pp. 51, 73, 96, 112. Cheit estimates that a "minimum growth" policy for higher education in the early 1970s will cost a plus 4 percent and that a "rock bottom" policy will cost plus 1 percent (p. 112).

- Other great priorities will remain before the nation.

- The labor market will experience an increasing surplus of some categories of college graduates and there will be less reason to subsidize a surplus.

- Students come increasingly from lower-income families less able to respond to higher and higher tuition as easily as do more affluent families with higher levels of disposable income. And middle-class elements are already resisting the public subsidy of college attendance by children of lower-income (including minority) families.

- The increasing magnitude of federal and state funds going into higher education draws more attention to this aspect of these budgets; and budget analysts are now more numerous and more skilled, and legislators and administrators are more concerned.

- The "adversary culture" may continue to find its most favorable environment on campus, and its greatest opposition in the general public.

- Growth in enrollments will continue to slow down from its historic rate of doubling every 10 to 15 years. In the 1980s there will be no increase at all. Bigger budgets were easier to obtain when justified by large enrollment increases; and will be harder to obtain when there are smaller or even no increases. A plus 2.5 percent cumulatively in the 1980s would mean an almost 30 percent increase in financial support over the decade (assuming no general inflation at all) with 0 percent increase in students.

Thus higher education faces a new situation. It has accomplished academic achievements in the past of great benefit to the nation; even some academic miracles. But the nation has changed and higher education has changed. Higher education must now be prepared again to accept a plus 2.5 percent or even less in the rate of increase in costs per student per year over the rate of general inflation. It must be more provident.

6 Higher education continues to perform essential functions and to have major claims on the resources of society:

- It must absorb about 3 million more students (on a full-time-equivalent basis) in the 1970s—about a 50 percent increase—but still equivalent to the total increase from 1636 to 1960; and increase the equality of opportunity as it does so.

- It must expand its research and service into new and complicated areas, including environmental protection and the renovation of urban life.

- It must provide a vast increase in health care personnel, on the order of one million persons in the 1970s.

Higher education must also reform itself and this, too, will cost money. It must improve its libraries, renovate general education, make its curriculum more relevant to the interest of students in the life of society and their place within it, expand its counseling services, increase the variety of its courses and programs in a number of institutions, experiment with the new technology, absorb more adult students, improve and expand its teaching services, work more closely with the high schools, provide even more student aid, make possible more early retirements, among many other things. And there is some slippage as the new replaces the old; some extra costs are involved in each turnaround—reform takes both time and money. Additionally, student interests are becoming more volatile as students seek new job opportunities and respond to new social interests[3] and, whether counted as reform or not, higher education will need to respond to those changing interests. Some fields will expand faster than others can be curtailed.

Thus higher education has some great new tasks to fulfill. This requires both new money and more effective use of existing resources.

7   A nearly $26-billion resource gap must be filled between 1970 and 1980. In 1970–71, institutions of higher education spent about $25 billion. In 1980–81, given a continuation of the trends of the 1960s in costs per student and in numbers of students, $51 billion will be needed even if there is no general inflation—which is highly unlikely. This $51 billion is a combination of about 50 percent more students and a cumulative increase in cost per student of 3.4 percent a year (the average annual increase in total current fund expenditures per full-time-equivalent student between 1959–60 and 1970–71). This potential increase, while very great, seems less phenomenal when it is realized that total expenditures more than tripled from 1960 to 1970, from $7.6 to $24.9 billion (in 1970–71 dollars).

8   How can this gap be closed?

We have earlier recommended vast increases in federal funding from $3.5 billion in 1967–68 to $12.5 billion in 1979–80 in constant dollars. We have recommended that the states raise their ef-

---

[3] See Richard E. Peterson, *American College and University Enrollment Trends in 1971* (publication pending by the Carnegie Commission on Higher Education).

fort per capita by one-quarter, from an average of about 0.80 percent of per capita income at the present time to an average of over 1.00 percent. We have also suggested that tuition charged to students and parents rise with the increase in per capita disposable income.

What can higher education do in addition to what should be done by the federal government, by the states, and by private individuals to reduce the gap? Two broad procedures are open to it: (1) reduce the total number of years of student training and (2) reduce the cost per student per year below what it otherwise might be. We believe that it can reduce expenditures in 1980 by about 10 percent by decreasing the length of time in college, and by about another 10 percent in a variety of other ways. This latter reduction can come at a rate of 1 percent a year adding up to about 10 percent by 1980. This is the same figure reached earlier by Howard Bowen in estimating the maximum savings that reasonably could be made.[4] This total of about 20 percent would reduce the costs incurred by institutions of higher education in 1980 to about $41.5 billion. Thus new funds would need to provide about $16.5 billion and more effective use of resources about $9.5 billion; the contribution of new money closing about 60 percent of the gap, and more effective use of resources about 40 percent.

New funds of $16.5 billion in the 1970s would almost match the new funds of about $17.3 billion in the 1960s (all in 1970–71 dollars). We believe that this is the maximum that can be expected. About 3 million more students on a full-time equivalent basis were added in the 1960s. About 3 million more will be added in the 1970s (although they need not spend so long on campus per student). It is unlikely that the 1970s will demonstrate any greater financial generosity to higher education than did the 1960s, and perhaps less; but we hope they may show about as much in total additional resources contributed in real terms. Higher education must prepare itself to live at least within these limits.

Saving nearly $10 billion a year by 1980 on the public and private bill for higher education seems like an enormous task. Taken year by year, it is much more manageable—1 percent through accelerated programs and 1 percent in other ways. Accelerated programs would reduce the number of students and application of the other

[4] "With best efforts, the scope for warranted cost-cutting will permit no more than 1 percent a year as an offset to the forces pushing costs upward" [Howard R. Bowen (4)].

methods would mean that costs per year per student would rise at 2.4 percent a year rather than at 3.4 percent. Putting the two together saves nearly $10 billion in 1980.

Some of this saving is already underway in many institutions. None of the above figures take general inflation into account. Inflation will raise all of these amounts, but the general line of argument will not be changed except that inflation adds greatly to the difficulties.

CHART 2 *Alternative patterns of growth in total current fund expenditures in higher education, in constant 1970–71 dollars*

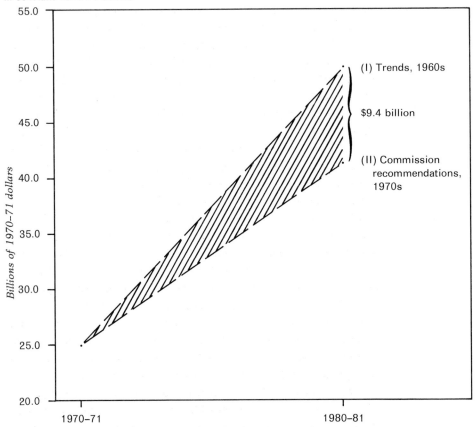

Academic year

NOTE: Alternative (I) assumes a growth rate in expenditures per FTE student of 3.4 percent per year from 1970–71 to 1980–81, and total FTE enrollment in 1980–81 of 9,756,000. Alternative (II) assumes a growth rate in expenditures per FTE student of 2.4 percent per year from 1970–71 to 1980–81, and total FTE enrollment in 1980–81 of 8,870,000 (90 percent of 9,756,000).

SOURCES: Computed from figures in the *Digest of Educational Statistics, 1970,* U.S. Office of Education; figures published in the *Chronicle of Higher Education,* April 17, 1972, p. 1; and from projections made by Gus W. Haggstrom, University of California, Berkeley.

Chart 2 shows *(a)* the situation if the trends of the 1960s are continued, *(b)* the situation if our recommendations to cut the number of student years through acceleration and to reduce the cost per student per year are followed, and *(c)* the gap between the two of $9.4 billion in 1980–81. Chart 3 is another way of looking at some of the data in Chart 2. Table 1 shows the situation in 1970–71 dollars *(a)* if costs per faculty member (rather than per student) were to accelerate as they did in the 1960s—4.2 per year in constant dollars, *(b)* if costs per student went up as they did in the 1960s—3.4 percent per year, *(c)* if costs per student rose at the

CHART 3 *New money for institutions of higher education (1970–71 dollars)*

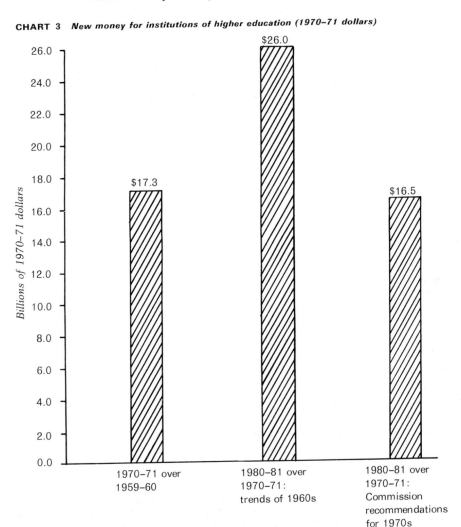

SOURCES: See Table 3.

"normal" long-term rate (1929–30 to 1959–60) — 2.5 percent, *(d)* if costs per student rose at our recommended rate of 2.4 percent, and *(e)* if, in addition to *(d)*, the number of student years is cut by 10 percent. Chart 2 relates *(b)* in this listing to *(e)*. Table 2 shows the additional effects of rates of general inflation of 2, 3, and 4 percent per year. Table 3 shows the percentage of the GNP spent on higher education including the 1.1 percent in 1959–60, the 2.5 percent at the present time, and several possibilities for 1980–81 ranging from 2.7 to 3.6 percent — our recommendations, as noted

TABLE 1 *Projections of total current fund expenditures in higher education from academic year 1970–71 to academic year 1980–81, using various growth rates and projected FTE enrollments* *

	Average annual percent growth rate	*Total FTE enrollment in 1980–81 (1,000's)*	*1980–81 expenditures (constant 1970–71 dollars)*	
			Total current fund expenditures per FTE student	*Total current fund expenditures ($ billions)*
(A) Rate of growth in total current fund expenditures per senior FTE faculty member, 1959–60 to 1970–71	4.2	9756	$5620	$54.8
Rate of growth in total current fund expenditures per FTE student,				
(B) 1959–60 to 1970–71	3.4	9756	$5203	$50.8
(C) 1929–30 to 1959–60	2.5	9756	$4762	$46.5
(D) Rate (B) minus 1.0	2.4	9756	$4721	$46.1
(E) Rate (B) minus 1.0	2.4	8780†	$4721	$41.4

*The projections are of total current fund expenditure per FTE student, from which projected total current fund expenditures are computed.

† 8780 is 90 percent of 9756.

SOURCES: Computed by Carnegie Commission staff from figures in the *Digest of Educational Statistics, 1970*, U.S. Office of Education, Washington, 1970, p. 99; from U.S. Office of Education figures published in the *Chronicle of Higher Education*, April 17, 1972, p. 2; from June O'Neill, *Resource Use in Higher Education*, Carnegie Commission on Higher Education, Berkeley, 1971, pp. 61, 62, 68; and from enrollment projections made by Gus W. Haggstrom, University of California, Berkeley.

TABLE 2 *Projections of total current fund expenditures in higher education from academic year 1970–71 to academic year 1980–81, using various growth rates in real expenditures and various rates of inflation**

				1980–81 expenditures (constant 1970–71 dollars)	
		Total FTE			
	Average annual percent real growth rate	*enrollment in 1980–81 (1,000's)*	*Average annual percent rate of general inflation*	*Total current fund expenditures per FTE student*	*Total current fund expenditures ($ billions)*
(A)	4.2	9,756	2.0	$6,790	$66.2
			3.0	7,460	72.7
			4.0	8,180	79.8
(B)	3.4	9,756	2.0	6,290	61.4
			3.0	6,920	67.5
			4.0	7,600	74.1
(C)	2.5	9,756	2.0	5,780	56.4
			3.0	6,350	62.0
			4.0	6,980	68.1
(D)	2.4	9,756	2.0	5,720	55.8
			3.0	6,290	61.4
			4.0	6,920	67.5
(E)	2.4	8,780*	2.0	5,720	50.2
			3.0	6,290	55.3
			4.0	6,920	60.7

* See footnotes in previous table.

NOTE: Letters (A) through (E) correspond to those in Table 1.

SOURCES: See Table 1.

earlier, would result in a figure of 2.7 percent. Chart 4 illustrates aspects of Table 3.

If expenditures of higher education were to hold at the current figure of 2.5 percent of the GNP throughout the 1970s, then expenditures in 1980–81 (in constant dollars) would be $38.1 billion or $13 billion more than the current level. We believe it is more reasonable to slow the rise in the percentage of the GNP from a possible 3.3 percent to a more realistic 2.7 percent rather than to hold to the current 2.5 percent. The task of adding another three million (FTE) students in the 1970s without reduction of academic quality will require some further modest increase in the percentage of the GNP.

9   Beyond these savings we believe that each institution of higher education should loosen up 1 to 3 percent of old funds each year to

	(1) *Total current fund expendi- ture in higher education*	(2) *Gross national product*	(3) *(1) as a percentage*
Year	*($ billions)*	*($ billions)*	*of (2)*
1959–60	7.6	666.5	1.1
1970–71	24.9	1010.5	2.5
1980–1981 (A)	54.8	1524.8	3.6
1980–1981 (B)	50.8	1524.8	3.3
1980–1981 (C)	46.5	1524.8	3.1
1980–1981 (D)	46.1	1524.8	3.0
1980–1981 (E)	41.4	1524.8	2.7

TABLE 3
*Total current
fund expenditure
in higher
education
relative to
gross national
product,
1959–60,
1970–71, and
projected
1980–81, in
constant
1970–71 dollars*

NOTE: Letters (A) through (E) correspond to those in Table 1.

SOURCES: Total current fund expenditures are from the *Digest of Educational Statistics, 1970,* U.S. Office of Education, Washington, 1971, p. 99; from U.S. Office of Education figures published in the *Chronicle of Higher Education,* April 17, 1972, p. 1; and from projections made by Carnegie Commission staff.

Gross national product is from *Economic Report of the President, 1972,* p. 195 (with 1959–60 data converted to 1970–71 dollars). The GNP has been projected to 1980–81 (in 1970–71 constant dollars) at an annual average rate of increase of 4.2 percent (a rate which is currently regarded as reasonable by economists).

CHART 4   *Alternative patterns of growth in the percent of GNP spent by institutions of higher education*

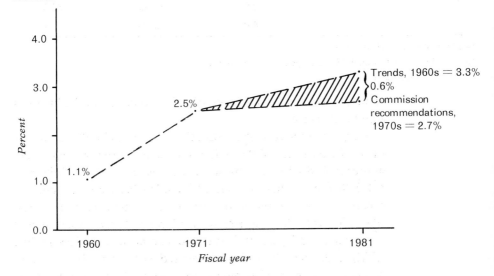

SOURCES: Total current fund expenditures from the *Digest of Educational Statistics, 1970.* U.S. Office of Education, Washington, 1971, p. 99; and from U.S. Office of Education figures published in the *Chronicle of Higher Education,* April 17, 1972, p. 1.

GNP is from the *Economic Report of the President,* Washington, 1971, pp. 95 and 197; and from the *Survey of Current Business,* February, 1972, p. S-1.

1981 projections are all by Carnegie Commission staff.

be used for self-renewal purposes—reforms and new programs. This will add to its dynamism as the new replaces the old. Our Commission has recommended many reforms in higher education and will recommend more. These reforms often cost money. Some of this money will need to come from new sources of funding, but some of it also can and should come from greater flexibility in the use of present funds. We place great emphasis on the reassignment of existing funds to new uses.

10 We are interested in these savings and in these funds for institutional renewal not only (1) to save resources for society and (2) to improve the vitality of institutions of higher education but particularly also (3) to assist students—by saving the time of students by reducing the years they spend in education, by reducing the duplication between high school and college they now endure, by making better use of their time in preparing them for the jobs that actually will exist and for enhancing the quality of their lives. These are the most important purposes of all. This can all be accomplished without any general reduction in academic quality. In fact, through greater emphasis on self-renewal, quality generally can be raised. But there will be marginal reductions in quality in some high cost areas in some institutions.

That the targets we set are reasonable is shown by the recent experience of such institutions as Princeton, Stanford, M.I.T., Case-Western Reserve and the University of California where much more has been accomplished recently on an annual basis than we recommend here.

Higher education must work on both sides of the equation—more money and more effective use of it. It should both obtain the money it really needs and maximize its output from this money. Constructive possibilities—not only negative ones—reside in a period of financial stringency. It is not enough to bemoan fate or to look to others for help; higher education must also help itself.

It may be argued that we do not yet know as much as we should know about the results of alternative actions. This is true. But still we must act in accordance with the knowledge we do have.

11 Some distinctions must be made. We have talked about the total public and private national bill for higher education. A second perspective is from the point of view of the expenditures of a campus; a third is the cost per student.

Different actions affect these differently. Accelerating education by one year, for example, will reduce the national bill; usually it will not reduce campus expenditures, however, since more students will be added to each class keeping the total constant; and for the student, the cost will be the same each year but there will be fewer years to pay for and one less year of foregone earnings. Year-round operations, as another example, will save on construction and on some other costs per student but will increase the campus operating budget if the same number of students are kept around the year.

Another distinction is between reducing total costs to the nation and merely shifting them around. For example, if the federal government takes over more of the cost of aid for students, this may reduce the contributions both of parents and of institutions but not total costs. Some redistribution of costs is highly desirable and we have strongly recommended it, but our particular interest in this report is in reducing the total bill and not just in shifting its burden.

A further distinction is between short-term savings and long-term savings. Reducing maintenance, for example, will save costs in the short-term but may well add to them in the long-term.

12   The principal sources we see for savings are as follows:

(1) Reducing the number of students by *(a)* accelerating programs and *(b)* reducing the number of reluctant attenders. We believe that the former will reduce operating costs by at least 10 and perhaps 15 percent, and capital costs, in the 1970s, by one third.

The latter *(b)* is an unknown factor. A substantial number of students (perhaps 5 to 15 percent or more) are reluctant attenders to one degree or another. The change in the draft has already reduced pressures for attendance. Students are becoming more independent in their actions as against parental pressures to attend college and peer-group pressures may also be becoming less in favor of attendance. Counseling can help reduce the reluctant attenders, as can limits on the years permitted as a graduate student, as can more frequent exit portals as provided by the Associate of Arts and Master of Philosophy degrees. A national service program, presumably, would also draw out some reluctant attenders. Full employment would help greatly. Employers also may start hiring for some jobs giving less preference to persons who have attended colleges. The Supreme Court, in its decision in *Griggs* v. *Duke Power Company* encourages practice in this direction. How much policy within higher education can help reduce the number of reluctant attenders it is impossible to know, but

- Research expenditures by the federal government are more likely to rise in the 1970s at the same rate as the GNP rather than at a rate two to three times that fast, as they did through most of the 1960s. If the same proportion of federal monies are spent through higher education, then total expenditures of higher education will rise less rapidly than in the 1960s. Federal funds for "academic science" (not counting federally supported R&D centers attached to universities) rose at an annual average rate of 10.6 percent in constant dollars from 1959–60 to 1970–71. The difference between that rate of increase continued throughout the 1970s and an increase tied to the estimated rate of increase of the GNP in real terms of 4.2 percent amounts to a total of $3 billion a year by 1980–81. We have recommended in earlier reports that federal research funds rise with the GNP in the future. If these funds do rise with the GNP instead of at the rate of over 10 percent per year of the past decade, then the resulting reductions in the total expenditures of higher education will amount to a little over 0.5 percent a year.

(4) Offsetting these savings will be costs external to higher education that result from policies we have recommended, such as:

- Absorption by the high schools of work now given in the first year of college.
- Better counseling in the high schools.
- Introduction of a full-scale national service program.

Many other savings are possible, but the big savings are noted under (1), (2) and (3) above. These are the areas where the greatest possibilities exist.

13   What not to do is as important as what to do. We consider it unwise, however tempting in the short-run, to cut such items as:

- Necessary maintenance
- Library expenditures for new books and for journals
- Student aid without at least making loans available

We also consider it unwise to keep down costs by excessive turnover of low-paid assistant professors.

We oppose, for reasons given below, state interference with internal budgetary details and arrangements — such as required teaching loads.

We counsel against federal "bail out" funds, but do favor short-term funds for development of size and of variety of programs on selected campuses into more viable long-term arrangements as through the federal "developing colleges" program.

Neither short-run expediency nor long-term external bureaucratic interference are effective solutions.

14   The 1980s will pose special problems. There will be no growth in enrollment, yet costs will rise substantially, as we have noted above, and the pressures to cut them will be intense.

One special problem will be the over-supply of new Ph.D.'s, particularly those who are white males. Few places will open up and many of these will go to qualified women and to members of minority groups.

Another special problem will confront the young assistant professors as higher ranks are already loaded with tenured faculty members.

One solution to these special problems may be to encourage the enrollment of adults in that decade. Another may be to let the student-faculty ratio rise in the 1970s and then to lower it in the 1980s—but this raises budgetary difficulties in the 1980s. A further one is to push early retirement plans, possibly combined with a partial work load. An additional possibility is to hire many part-time lecturers in the 1970s, holding some permanent positions open to be filled in the 1980s.

The combination of no total growth in enrollment plus the possible continued volatility of students in choice of fields argues for the greatest possible flexibility. It will be a difficult decade. It merits some advance thought.

15   Beyond the 1980s there will still be problems. Two possibilities that are particularly important are (1) a continuing high income elasticity of demand for higher education so that comparative costs can keep on rising indefinitely without curtailing demand—but someday a plateau of resistance may be encountered since plus 2.5 or even plus 2 percent a year accumulates very rapidly, and (2) the new electronic technology which by the year 2000 may be able to reduce unit costs for some aspects of administration, library operation, and instruction quite substantially. The quick sources of solutions to financial problems, however, will, by the year 2000, have been exhausted; for example, moving to year-round operations or to a three-year B.A. degree happens only once.

16 Some comments on the process of getting more effective use of resources are in order:

(1) It will cause conflicts—of department versus department, of faculty against administration, of administration versus state authorities. Costs will confront quality; the new will challenge the old; the welfare of the total institution will battle against the status quo of its component parts. Unionization becomes more likely as faculty members face some unpleasant changes, as they seek to defend what they have or what they have come to expect. Consensus is more likely when the struggle over money is less intense.

(2) It will cause a greater degree of centralization of authority on campus—perhaps also in the coordinating council or the state government. Administration, whether inside or outside, gains authority because it deals with money and money is now particularly important. Also, many of the policies that save money, such as avoidance of duplication of effort, must be made and enforced centrally. Administration in academic life rightfully is a means not an end. Under these circumstances, however, it may come to seem and even sometimes to be that the means determine the ends.

(3) For both of the above reasons, governance becomes more difficult to arrange and to manage.

(4) The necessary changes take time. Budgets are made each year, and each year the budget authorities may press harder than the academic institutions can readily accept. The adjustments are much more easily made over a decade than in one single year.

17 The campus is a peculiar type of institution. It has been run, in its academic aspects, quite properly, with a professional mentality toward standards. But the academic profession has been one whose members do not directly subject their wares to a market test. Other professionals (doctors, lawyers) also have a professional mentality, but they are more in touch with the market for their services. The faculty, in a great majority of academic institutions, is in control of or has strong influence over teaching loads, courses, research projects, class sizes, admissions, grades, degrees—over its own work loads and its own products. The administration, however, raises the money. The people who spend the money do not raise it, and the people who raise it have only modest influence over how it is spent. This disjunction is a source of problems. It is hard both to assess responsibility (to the administration or to the faculty?) and to affect results (by global actions or by specific controls?). The campus is like an independent artisan economy from the point of view of producing services but it is a collective enterprise in terms of securing income—and the chief artisans have tenure. The president has little control over the component outputs or the totality to which they add up, but he must take the totality and present it for the highest price he can get in a market where there is often only one big purchaser—the state. It is not like a corporation with hierarchical control over employees nor like a government agency. Comparisons with either are false and can lead to unwise policies.

Current attempts to solve some problems peculiar to higher education include an effort to turn the communal artisan endeavor into a public utility enterprise—to determine its prices, specify its output, assign its customers to it by public fiat; to impose more and more specific financial formulas controlling income in detail; to set work loads and class sizes; to manage the enterprise by remote control. There are several things wrong with this: (1) Outputs are difficult to specify and quantify. (2) Many services are performed by many different people in many different combinations—the diversity of effort is almost infinite. (3) Morale is at the essence of the enterprise and it is founded on self-determination of effort and self-generated goals. (4) The campus can become a perfect environment for the "Good Soldier Schweik" who follows all the rules but cleverly sabotages the whole endeavor.

The problem is complex. The essence of the solution lies in conditions that *(a)*draw forth the maximum of voluntary effort at a high level of competence and *(b)* achieve effective use of resources. The artisan approach generally satisfies *(a)*. Faculty members do work hard (a few abuses aside) and some of their contributions in teaching and research have been superb. This kind of performance can neither be controlled in detail nor coerced. It has been a productive form of mild anarchy—internal free enterprise. The spirit of the enterprise can be killed by driving the public utility approach farther and farther into the details of the operation. We support continued faculty responsibility for the essentials of academic life.

But achieving effective use of resources remains a problem. How can it be achieved while preserving the spirit of the academic enterprise? We see the solutions in (1) general tests of performance and general formulas for support by the state; (2) greater reliance on the market, such as:

(a) Money received through the hands of the students, as now is the case of private colleges and universities—let them conduct the search for lower costs, higher quality and greater diversity

(b) Auxiliary enterprises placed on a self-supporting basis or turned over to independent enterprises

(c) Research funds given out by panels of experts on a project by project basis in competition with each other

(3) greater self-discipline within the academic enterprise, a greater sense of responsibility for effective use of resources—much has been left to the conscience of the academic community but this conscience now needs better ways to inform itself and to assert itself. We believe it is important to preserve the essential quality of and thus the essential faculty responsibility for academic life. It is also important to realize what different kinds of external pressures both can and cannot do—they can guide but they cannot coerce effort. The Procrustean bed is not a productive instrument in academic life; and yet we have been moving in that direction.

18 Self-discipline at the institutional level can be aided by:

(1) Improving the budget-making process. We suggest that the budget assign total costs to each endeavor (including rentals for space and equipment—there is little incentive to save on what are "free" goods); that it consolidate consideration of capital and operating budgets so that the impact of each on the other can better be seen and trade-offs can be made—for example, in considering year-round operations; that it look at the long-term and not just the individual year; that it concentrate more on outputs and less exclusively on inputs, and particularly more on "value added."

(2) Obtaining better data and making it more widely available within the academic community. It is particularly important to have *(a)* global cost and output data among institutions of comparable quality and with comparable endeavors and *(b)* specific cost and output data among departments within the same institution. Quality is of the essence in academic life and it is hard to measure; but among carefully selected institutions and within the same institution it may be assumed to be sufficiently equal so that comparisons can be made—it is easier to compare quality than it is to measure it. But even within these restricted limits great care must be taken in making comparisons; they are a starting point but not the end point of

proper consideration. The best measure of output is student credit hours—for example, student credit hours per $1,000. "Data pools" can be helpful—like the ACE studies of quality at the graduate level. Regional associations also can be helpful in creating them and some, in particular the SREB in the South and WICHE in the West, are. The U.S. Office of Education has a particular responsibility in regard to cost and output data. Consortia, as among certain private colleges in Pennsylvania, can also be helpful in gathering and exchanging data.

The information system is now very poor in higher education.

(3) Maximizing flexibility in creation of space and in making commitments to people. This assists the process of necessary change. New projects should be on a trial basis; faculty members with tenure should be a reasonable proportion of the total instructional staff; early retirement on a part-time or full-time basis should be possible; young faculty members should be hired with regard to their adaptability to future assignments—the young faculty members hired in 1972 will retire in the year 2012; certain of the positions vacated should be recaptured for central reassignment; and so forth.

(4) Setting a quota of "liberated" money each year, as suggested above, perhaps 1 to 3 percent. This money, taken from old assignments either on an across-the-board or selective basis, can then be used for reform, for new projects, for meeting the more volatile career and academic interests of students. Some old activities should be stopped altogether.

(5) Having a competent central staff with adequate authority.

(6) Creating incentives to save. The state can share savings with the campus rather than demand them all and thus make them disappear. The faculty can be assured benefits from savings, for example, some proportion might be assigned to salary increases or library purchases; and also the students—for example, more money for student aid or lower tuition increases. Faculty and students will need to share in some advisory role in budget making for these incentives to be fully effective.

The only way to keep faculty salaries ahead of the cost of living, to improve the library, to get more money for scholarships, to keep down increases in tuition, to get academic reform may be to make other adjustments in resource use. Hard choices must be made. Incentives can help both in making them and gaining their acceptance.

(7) Convincing the faculty of the need to be more cost conscious. The severity of the new situation is not as yet always fully appreciated. The 1960s were an unusual period; not par for the academic course. Salaries cannot keep rising so fast on a comparative basis; teaching loads may have to be increased instead of reduced; facilities and amenities cannot be so significantly improved; new Ph.D. programs cannot so readily be added.

For many institutions survival is at stake; for all, a confrontation with public support already exists.

But only so much can be done. One rule is that it is easier to manage things in academic life, than people—to save on things, to centralize control of their use. Another rule is that effective use of resources is a political as well as a technical problem. From a political point of view, outside pressure helps—from the market or from the state budget authority provided it is reasonable in amount and general in form. Across-the-board cuts are easier than selective cuts. Cuts are best offset by some generalized gains for the participants. Consultants can ease action by taking responsibility for difficult recommendations. Good data, widely distributed, are essential. People should not be taken by surprise—consultation and hearings are a part of the educational process. The economies of the situation can only be handled well as the politics are conducted with care and consideration.

19   Who should do what? We suggest that:

- *The federal government*   be restrictive in extending support to new Ph.D. programs; concentrate its research effort in the most productive institutions; extend funds as much as possible through student aid and related cost-of-education allowances; aid small institutions to expand their size and extend their programs; continue its bonus for accelerated programs for medical physicians and dentists (and extend this approach where appropriate); greatly expand its national service program for youth; collect better cost data through the Office of Education; finance experimentation with the new technology.

- *The states*   (and their coordinating councils) base budgets on broad formulas that consider quality and quantity of output and costs among comparable institutions; provide bonuses for accelerated degree programs; set standards for optimum size of each type of campus; share savings with institutions; support private institutions to a reasonable extent and in reasonable ways; encourage year-round operations if only by looking at year-round utilization rates among campuses when deciding where new construction is most justified; provide for differentiation of functions among systems and campuses; support the extension of the D.A. degree; inaugurate "open" universities on a state or regional basis; and look at the general situation and leave the detailed adjustments to the campus.

- *Trustees*   request data, at least annually, on outputs and costs as compared with similar institutions on a global basis and as among departments internally on a more specific basis; review policies that affect costs in major ways; review policies on budgetary flexibility and the recapturing and reassignment of old funds; examine the student-faculty ratio; assign adequate authority and staff to the office of the president.

- *The president* provide the data the Board needs and the review of policies and procedures; cooperate in starting and using consortia; accept basic responsibility for effective use of resources and generally serve as the leader of the faculty and the trustees in assuring the effective use of resources.

- *The faculty* recognize that a new situation has arisen that requires more effective use of total resources and more flexible assignment of them; protect their essential responsibility for the quality of the academic enterprise; give careful consideration to work loads, number of courses, size of classes, tenure percentages; create exit portals at the Associate of Arts and Master of Philosophy levels; accept the D.A. degree; scrutinize the educational impact of financial actions.

- *The high schools* prepare to absorb work now given in the first year of college; improve their counseling services.

Moving from trajectory I of the 1960s to trajectory II for the 1970s is a difficult process involving the contributions and the understanding of a substantial number of people and groups. Expectations rose in the 1960s and this was comparatively easy. The reverse is not. A "revolution of rising expectations" is hard enough to experience; one of "disappointed expectations" is even more so.

20 The problem of the effective use of resources will be with higher education for a long time. But then higher education has lived with this problem for most of its over 300 years of history. What is different today is not the existence of the problem but rather its current shape and its intensity. An enormous resource gap exists for the 1970s. The basic choice is whether we just drift through it or whether we try to master it. How can higher education reach 1980 in the best possible academic condition, with the least possible damage due to financial stringency?

2. Dimensions of the Financial Crisis

The general outlines of the financial crisis that began to develop in the late 1960s are becoming widely familiar as more and more studies of the situation are published. Earl Cheit's intensive study of the financial position of 41 institutions, conducted for the Commission in 1970 (5), indicated that less than one-third of these institutions were "not in financial trouble" at the time of his study. Slightly more than two-fifths were classified as "headed for financial trouble" and more than one-fourth were deemed to be "in financial difficulty."

Cheit found that private colleges and universities were considerably more likely to be in financial difficulty in the spring of 1970 than their public counterparts and that, among types of institutions, universities and liberal arts colleges were especially likely to be facing financial troubles.

An Association of American Colleges study of 554 private colleges and universities indicated that the proportion with deficits on current-fund account rose from about 34 percent of the reporting institutions in 1967–68 to about 47 percent in 1970–71, while the combined deficits of the institutions that were "in the red" rose from $36 million in the former year to $87 million in the latter year (6). These amounts were not large in relation to the combined current-fund expenditures of institutions included in the study, but the trend was ominous. A year later, a follow-up study of the same group of institutions showed that the average private college had underestimated its 1969–70 deficit by nearly 25 percent and that the average deficit in 1970–71 was expected to be nearly eight times larger than two years earlier (7, p. 1).

In the fall of 1971 the financial status of public institutions of higher education also appeared to be deteriorating rapidly. Nearly two-thirds of the 55 early respondents to a survey by the National

Association of State Universities and Land-Grant Colleges reported "standstill" total budgets or less for 1971–72, while about one-half reported "standstill" state appropriations (8). The association estimated that to cover rising costs and increasing enrollments, a university should have an average annual increase of 10 percent in its operating budget to maintain its current level of services. Thus a "standstill" budget was one which reflected an increase of less than 10 percent. Especially serious was the problem of three state university systems with no increase in their state appropriations and nine state institutions or systems with a decrease in their appropriations (Appendix A, Table A-1).

As the dimensions of the crisis are becoming familiar, the factors underlying the financial difficulties of higher education are also beginning to be well understood.

Among the more important factors affecting *both public and private institutions* are the following:

1 From the beginning of the 1960s to about 1967–68, not only were enrollments rising rapidly, but so was income. The pronounced increase in federal funds made available for research and development encouraged rapid expansion of research and graduate training in universities, the assumption of portions of faculty salaries by research budgets, and the acquisition of expensive and complex equipment. Foundation funds were also forthcoming on a very substantial scale during this period. Civil rights pressure and growing concern over equality of opportunity led to substantial increases in federal funds, and also to significant increases in funds from state and private sources, for student aid. In addition, civil rights pressure stimulated the development of ethnic studies programs, while more open-admission standards created a need for remedial education. Other forces, such as the growing concern over urban issues and environmental problems, led to the development of new programs.

Also contributing to rapidly rising expenditures were the rising ratio of graduate enrollment to total enrollment, the growing use of computers, the increasing complexity of other equipment—especially in the natural sciences, rapidly rising library costs, the tendency to expand student services, expenses associated with episodes of student unrest, and rising security costs.

2 A growing and ominous imbalance between the rate of increase in income and the rate of increase in budgetary needs began in about 1967–68. Expenditures on higher education were rising as a percentage of the gross national product—from about 1 percent at the beginning of the 1960s to

more than 2 percent at the end of the decade — but appropriations for higher education were encountering increased competition with other needs that were considered more pressing and more urgent at both the federal and state levels. For these and other reasons, the flow of federal funds for both research and student aid tended to level off from about 1967–68 on. Certain foundation programs providing fellowship and other types of aid were also being phased out.

3 Meanwhile, the rate of inflation accelerated. Whereas the consumer price index rose at an annual average rate of 1.7 percent from 1960 to 1967, it increased at an annual average rate of 5.1 percent in the following three years. Salaries of faculty and nonfaculty personnel had to be increased rapidly just to keep their real incomes from declining, whereas earlier in the decade they had enjoyed substantial increases in real income.

4 Many of the universities with medical schools were encountering a problem of growing medical school deficits, which in some cases were draining funds from the parent institutions.

Of special importance for *public colleges and universities* were the following factors:

1 Governors and state legislatures were increasingly reluctant to support large increases in appropriations for public institutions of higher education, attributable in part to public concern over student unrest but also in large part to the increasing fiscal problems of state governments, which have been associated especially with inadequate tax structures on the revenue side and with mounting welfare costs on the expenditure side.

2 Voters were increasingly reluctant to approve bond issues for construction of needed facilities, again attributable in part to concern over student unrest. And, affecting community colleges, in particular, was the growing reluctance of voters, in the face of rapid increases in property and other local taxes, to approve needed tax increases in junior college districts.

Private institutions were especially affected by the following developments:

1 The growing tuition gap, in dollar terms, between public and private institutions, was making it increasingly difficult for many of the private institutions to compete for students. Private institutions are much more heavily dependent on tuition than are the traditionally low-tuition public institutions, and the accelerated increases in cost of education per student

have required accelerated increases in tuition in recent years. Between 1967–68 and 1971–72 (estimated) tuition and fees rose at an annual average rate of 8.6 percent, as compared with an annual average rate of 6.7 percent in the previous four-year period, in private institutions of higher education. Tuition and fees at public institutions rose at nearly as rapid a rate in the later four-year period, but, because tuition and fees at public institutions are so much lower than those at private colleges and universities, the dollar gap widened—from $778, on the average, in 1963–64 to $1,035 in 1967–68 to $1,447 in 1971–72.[1]

And, if we consider the more selective private institutions, where the "going" rate of tuition is approaching $3,000 a year, and compare their tuition with those of their most nearly comparable public counterparts, we find a tuition gap of well over $2,000. Meanwhile per capita disposable income has not been rising as rapidly in recent years as have tuition charges in private institutions. The problem of the growing tuition gap is especially serious for some of the large urban universities, such as St. Louis University, Tulane University, and New York University.

2   Because of greatly increased emphasis on equality of opportunity, there was a pronounced tendency for private colleges and universities to increase the amounts of funds allocated to student aid each time tuition was increased, in order not to make it increasingly difficult for low-income and disadvantaged students to enroll. A substantial factor in explaining the growing deficits of many private colleges was the growing gap between the availability of (restricted) funds intended specifically for student aid and the amounts actually made available from all sources for student aid.

3   Over the decades, as total enrollment in private higher education has increased, there has been a tendency for endowment income to decline in relative importance as a source of revenue for private colleges and universities. With the rapid increase in enrollment that occurred during the early part of the 1960s, this tendency was accentuated. Meanwhile, the stock market decline in the late 1960s adversely affected opportunities of institutions to benefit from capital gains. However, private gifts to all colleges and universities held up very well through most of the 1960s and rose especially sharply (15 percent) between 1967–68 and 1968–69. In view of the recession in the following year, it was not particularly surprising that there was a slight drop in private giving. New federal tax restrictions and the reaction to campus unrest also played a role in accounting for the decline, according to the Council for Financial Aid to Education (9).

[1] The figures relate to the difference between average tuition at private institutions and average tuition for state residents at public institutions. Differences are much smaller between tuition at private institutions and tuition for students from out of the state at public institutions.

Some commentators have pointed out, quite rightly, that a financial crisis in higher education does not exist in the sense that any substantial number of institutions are faced with bankruptcy. But there is surely a crisis in the sense that many private institutions would reach the point of bankruptcy in the not too distant future if their deficits continued to grow as they have in recent years, and many public institutions would increasingly be forced to reduce quality and/or turn away qualified students if they continued to be denied adequate increases in state appropriations for a number of years.

All the available evidence suggests that the financial problems of institutions of higher education are likely to continue to be serious, at least until the mid-1970s and most likely far beyond that time.

Already the financial crisis has forced many institutions of higher education to curb increases in expenditures. Some have taken great care to assure that expenditures might be pruned in ways that would be least harmful to the quality of education. We shall have more to say about the economies they have achieved in later sections. But too often the pattern is one of across-the-board cost-cutting, such as deferred maintenance, a general freeze on hiring, uniform budget cuts for all departments, and, in public institutions, restrictions on the enrollment of qualified students. Some of these measures, such as deferred maintenance, may help in the short run but merely exacerbate problems in the long run, as costs rise (10, pp. 125–126). A general freeze on hiring may, unless it is administered with some degree of flexibility, have undesirable repercussions in a situation in which there is a need for expansion in some fields and contraction in others in response to the dramatic changes that are occurring in the job market for college graduates.

There is an acute need for all colleges and universities that are faced with the necessity to economize to turn from the kinds of emergency measures that have been widely adopted thus far to more carefully considered selective economies. At the same time, the search for effective use of resources in higher education should not be regarded purely as a response to the current financial crisis. Interest in analyzing ways of achieving more effective use of resources in higher education began to develop long before the onset of the financial crisis and is an important and necessary development in higher education quite apart from the impact of the crisis. The Commission believes that, even if the financial crisis were to abate in the relatively near future, the effort to achieve more effective use of resources should continue to receive very substantial emphasis in institutions of higher education. There are, indeed, some positive benefits in the current fiscal crisis, as well as grave liabilities. Not only are more and more institutions being forced to find ways of bringing costs under more effective control, but colleges and universities — especially those that are privately controlled — are coming together as never before to analyze their mutual situations, seek increased federal and state aid, and study ways in which they might achieve economies through interinstitutional cooperation. Thus, although the present period is a painful one for those who are responsible for balancing the budgets of institutions of higher education, and some of the emergency cost-cutting that is going on is jeopardizing quality in the affected institutions, there is little question that there will be long-run net benefits in the form not only of more effective institutional management but also, perhaps, of more effective sharing of resources among groups of institutions.

3. The Behavior of Costs

Higher education is a labor-intensive service sector of the economy in which it is difficult to achieve the gains in productivity that are experienced in goods-producing industries. In this respect it is much like other service sectors. A Mark Hopkins can certainly have more than one student at the other end of his log, but there is also great value in the type of interchange between faculty and students that is possible in small classes. Even as we move, albeit slowly, toward televised and computerized instruction, we realize that large amounts of faculty input are required if such methods are to be successful.

In the goods-producing sectors of the economy, inflationary increases in costs are to some degree offset by gains in productivity, but this is relatively unlikely in service sectors. For purposes of historical comparisons of educational costs, the most useful data are those compiled by June O'Neill in a study conducted for the Carnegie Commission (Table 4). Educational costs per credit hour consistently rose more rapidly than the consumer price index from 1953–54 to 1966–67. Over the period as a whole, educational costs rose at an annual average rate of 3.5 percent, as compared with a rate of 1.6 percent for the consumer price index—a difference of 1.9 percent. However, costs in private institutions of higher education rose more sharply than those in public institutions. The rate of increase for private institutions was 4.8 percent, or 3.2 percent more than the consumer price index, and for public institutions, 2.9 percent, or only 1.3 percent more than the consumer price index. For higher education as a whole, the excess of 1.9 percent over the average annual increase in the consumer price index during this period was somewhat less than the 2.5 percent shown by the O'Neill data for the period 1929–30 to 1959–60 (Table 1).

The difference in behavior of costs between public and private institutions was particularly pronounced for the universities,

		1953–54 to 1957–58	1957–58 to 1963–64	1963–64 to 1966–67	1953–54 to 1966–67
TABLE 4 Annual average rate of increase in educational costs per credit hour, in institutions of higher education, by type and control, and in consumer price index, selected periods, 1953–54 to 1966–67	**Institutions by control and type**				
	All institutions	2.8%	3.9%	3.8%	3.5%
	Public	2.0	3.1	3.8	2.9
	Universities	1.9	3.8	3.5	3.1
	Other four-year institutions	2.4	2.3	4.4	2.8
	Two-year institutions	1.7	3.5	6.3	3.6
	Private	4.0	5.5	4.4	4.8
	Universities	4.4	6.9	4.8	5.6
	Other four-year institutions	3.5	5.0	4.5	4.4
	Two-year institutions	8.7	1.7	1.5	3.7
	Consumer price index	1.6	1.3	2.2	1.6

SOURCE: Computed from data in June O'Neill, *Resource Use in Higher Education: Trends in Output and Inputs, 1930 to 1967,* Carnegie Commission on Higher Education, Berkeley, Calif., 1971, p. 43.

especially in the first two sub-periods shown in Table 4. A major explanation was a substantial increase in the ratio of graduate enrollment (with its relatively high costs) to total enrollment in private universities, whereas this was happening only to a slight extent in public universities. And, as we shall see, costs of graduate education were rising more sharply than costs of undergraduate education.

Another important factor explaining the less pronounced rise in costs in public higher education was the sharp increase in the share of total enrollment in public two-year colleges (11, pp. 25 and 28), which tend to have relatively low costs. On the other hand, enrollment in private two-year colleges has tended to level off in recent years, and there is evidence that many of these institutions have particularly severe financial problems. After a sharp increase in the first sub-period represented in Table 4, their costs rose relatively little subsequently, suggesting that they were struggling to hold expenditures in line in order to avoid tuition increases that would exacerbate their difficulties in competing with public two-year colleges for enrollment.

The difference in the rate of cost increases between public and

TABLE 5 Annual average rate of increase in weighted* costs per FTE student in institutions of higher education, by control, and in consumer price index, selected periods, 1959–60 to 1969–70

Control of institution— educational costs per student, and consumer price index	1959–60	1963–64	1966–67	1969–70	1959–60 to 1969–70
All institutions					
Educational costs per FTE student*	$1,007	$1,173	$1,411	$1,772	
Annual average increase		3.9%	6.3%	7.9%	5.8%
Public					
Educational costs per student*	$1,018	$1,110	$1,301	$1,659	
Annual average increase		2.2%	5.4%	8.4%	5.0%
Private					
Educational costs per student*	$990	$1,282	$1,641	$2,070	
Annual average increase		6.7%	8.6%	8.0%	7.7%
Consumer price index (1967 = 100)	88.0	92.3	98.6	113.1	
Annual average increase		1.2%	2.2%	4.7%	2.5%

*Includes instruction and departmental research; extension and public service; libraries; general administration, general institutional expense, and student services; organized activities relating to educational departments; other sponsored programs; and all other educational and general expense. In computing all averages, graduate FTE enrollment is given a weight of three, as compared with a weight of one for undergraduate FTE enrollment.

SOURCE: Adapted from U.S. Office of Education data by the Carnegie Commission staff.

private higher education tended to narrow during the course of the 1960s, and in the last three years for which data are available, the rate of increase was actually slightly lower for private than for public institutions (Table 5). Here, as in subsequent tables, we have given graduate FTE enrollment a weight of three, as compared with undergraduate FTE enrollment, to reflect its higher costs, which will be discussed more fully at a later point. During these years, many private colleges and universities were beginning their efforts to combat rising deficits, whereas public institutions for the most part were not yet facing the severe budgetary constraints that were to develop in the early 1970s. But both public and private institutions were facing an accelerated rate of increase in the consumer price index—a factor which largely explained the relatively high rate of increase in costs for higher education as a whole during this three-year period.

The data in Table 5, reflecting more recent developments than those in Table 4, indicate that during the 1960s educational costs per FTE student in higher education as a whole rose at an annual average rate that was 3.3 percent higher than the rate of increase in the consumer price index. For private institutions the difference was 5.2 percent, and for public institutions it was 2.5 percent. The 3.3 percent excess for higher education as a whole differs slightly from the 3.4 percent shown in Table 1, which is based on the period from 1959–60 to 1970–71 and in which data on FTE enrollment have not been weighted as they have been in Table 5.

As already suggested, the cost of education per FTE student is considerably higher at the graduate than at the undergraduate level; it is also higher for upper-division than for lower-division under-graduates. Studies of comparative costs have been conducted at a number of institutions in the United States and Canada, yielding roughly similar results. For example, a study of credit-hour costs per student in public higher education in Oklahoma indicated that upper-division costs were higher than lower-division costs in both science and nonscience, but that the difference was wider in science, undoubtedly because costly laboratory equipment plays a relatively greater role in upper-division than in lower-division science (Table 6). Graduate education was several times more costly than undergraduate education, but again the difference was much wider in science. Rates of increase in costs from 1961–62 to 1966–67 were considerably higher for all graduate education and for upper-division science than for other divisions.

On the average, graduate education has been estimated to be about three times as costly as undergraduate education at both the University of California and the University of Toronto. The ratio at Princeton is 2.5 to 1, but educational expenditures per student in undergraduate education are considerably higher at Princeton than at either California or Toronto. Advanced graduate education is also considerably more costly than training at the master's level.

Another familiar aspect of the behavior of costs in higher education is the fact that library costs and computer costs have been rising considerably more rapidly than other components of costs, and these particular costs are especially great at the graduate level.

In view of the differences in cost by level of instruction we would expect variations by type of institution, depending on their "mix"

TABLE 6 Ratio of credit hour costs per student at various levels of public higher education in Oklahoma to average costs for all divisions, 1961–62 and 1966–67	Level of instruction	Ratios		Percentage increase in credit hour costs
		1961–62	*1966–67*	
	All divisions	1.00	1.00	21
	Lower division science	0.76	0.79	26
	Lower division nonscience	0.75	0.71	14
	Upper division science	1.24	1.51	47
	Upper division nonscience	1.13	1.11	19
	Graduate science	3.79	4.50	44
	Graduate nonscience	2.34	2.72	40

SOURCE: Computed from data in J. Froomkin, *Enrollments and Resources: The Challenge to Higher Education in the Seventies*, U.S. Office of Education, Washington, 1970, p. 41.

of levels (Table 7). Costs (measured by educational and general expense less expenses for organized research per FTE student) tend to be higher in private than in public institutions, but there are exceptions—other doctoral-granting universities I and liberal arts colleges II.

In general, expenditures per FTE student tend to decline as we proceed from highly research-oriented universities to universities with less emphasis on research to comprehensive colleges and universities. Expenditures per student tend to be higher in liberal arts colleges I (the more selective of these colleges) than in comprehensive colleges and universities, but interestingly there is relatively little difference in expenditures per student on this weighted basis between the latter group and two-year institutions.

Geographic location also affects cost in both public and private institutions, with relatively high costs, especially for faculty and nonfaculty salaries, prevailing in institutions in large urban areas.

There are economies of scale in higher education, but their effects are often muted by other influences which tend to result in rising costs with increasing enrollment.[1] The chief of these other influences is a tendency for institutions to add new fields of instruction

[1] An earlier discussion of economies of scale was included in the Commission's report, *New Students and New Places* (1971).

TABLE 7		Public			
	Type of institution	Educational and general expense† (less organized research)	Instruction and departmental research	Organized research	Student aid
Universities					
	Research universities I	$2,114	$976	$728	$63
	Research universities II	$1,704	836	614	86
	Other doctoral-granting universities I	1,872	929	400	64
	Other doctoral-granting universities II	1,279	701	166	48
Comprehensive colleges and universities					
	Comprehensive colleges and universities I	1,171	660	23	46
	Comprehensive colleges and universities II	1,131	655	6	56
Liberal arts colleges					
	Liberal arts colleges I §	0	0	0	0
	Liberal arts colleges II	1,684	732	4	72
	Two-year institutions	1,041	609	0	18

TABLE 7 Weighted annual expenditures per FTE student, by selected types of expense and by type and control of institution, United States, 1967–68*

* Includes United States and outlying areas; excludes institutions that did not report financial data; specialized institutions are excluded, since their costs vary widely by type of institution (medical, engineering, etc.).

† Includes instruction and departmental research; extension and public service; libraries; general administration, general institutional expense, and student services; organized activities relating to educational departments; other sponsored programs; and all other educational and general expense. In computing all averages, graduate FTE enrollment is given a weight of three, as compared with a weight of one for undergraduate FTE enrollment.

—often in relatively expensive fields such as science and engineering—as they grow in size. This factor is especially significant in universities, comprehensive colleges, and community colleges (with relatively high costs per student in such fields as engineering technology and allied health professions in community colleges).

Our data on the relationship of costs to enrollment, presented in Appendix C, indicate that there are economies of scales in administrative, library, and plant maintenance costs—in fact, for some groups of institutions, economies of scale are more clearcut in these categories than in instructional costs.

	Private		
Educational and general expense (less organized research)	Instruction and departmental research	Organized research	Student aid
$2,794‡	$1,189‡	$2,384‡	$279‡
2,236	906	779	226
1,449	831	308	72
1,530	810	233	71
1,252	623	32	61
1,343	620	36	50
2,367	1,112	57	184
1,556	701	8	82
1,477	592	2	62

‡ Excludes two institutions in this group with relatively small student bodies and exceptionally high expenditures per student.
§ There are no public institutions in this category.
SOURCE: Adapted from U.S. Office of Education data by the Carnegie Commission staff. For a description of the Carnegie Commission classification of institutions used here, see Carnegie Commission on Higher Education, *New Students and New Places*, McGraw-Hill Book Company, New York, 1971, Appendix A.

Our data also indicate that, although there is some evidence of a general tendency for educational costs per FTE student to decline with increasing enrollment, there are wide differences in cost per student among similar institutions of approximately the same size.[2] These wide variations in expenditure per student tend to be explained by differences in income per student. Long-established, selective, private universities and colleges tend to have more endowment income than less selective private institutions, as well as

[2] This was revealed in the scatter diagrams published in ibid., pp. 70–80.

greater success in attracting gifts from alumni and other private sources. Variations in expenditures per student among public institutions tend to be explained by differences in allocation per student made available by state legislatures, but there are also other factors at work. The University of Michigan, for example, has more income per student than the University of Illinois partly because of its higher tuition charge for state residents and partly because it has a far higher proportion of out-of-state students who pay much higher tuition than do residents of the state. The relation of expenditures and income is not coincidental of course; if the income did not come in, the expenditure could not be made.

As Howard Bowen (4) and others have pointed out, colleges and universities strive to maximize their resources, and then they spend what they receive. Thus, a major explanation of cost variations among similar institutions of similar size is the difference in their capacity to attract income. On the basis of a study of liberal arts colleges, Robert Heller and Associates described two "prestige" colleges, both enrolling just under 1,000 students, with costs, respectively, of $4,380 and $2,740 per student in 1969. The study revealed that the high cost college had a considerably larger faculty. The substantial difference in costs per student appears to be explained by the higher income-generating capacity of the high cost college (12). These differing levels of costs for institutions of about the same size and quality imply that major reductions in cost can occur on some campuses.

To suggest that differences in expenditures per student are largely explained by variations in the relative capacities of colleges and universities to attract income is not to deny that relatively high expenditures for students are likely to be associated with comparatively high quality. The universities with outstandingly high ratings in the studies of graduate education conducted by the American Council on Education (13 and 14), for example, are heavily concentrated in our Research Universities I group, in which educational expenditures per FTE student are relatively high (Table 7). Similarly, the relatively selective private liberal arts colleges — Liberal Arts I — tend to be those which have reputations for high quality, and their average expenditures per student are well above those of Liberal Arts Colleges II. In other words, the institutions that can attract relatively large amounts of income per student can afford to pay relatively high faculty salaries, maintain relatively high faculty-student ratios, spend more on their libraries, and in other ways provide a more stimulating intellectual environment for their students. But this does not necessarily mean that cost differences among institutions—or among particular programs within institutions—invariably reflect differences in quality.

The Commission has recommended that state plans for the growth and development of public institutions of higher education should, in general, incorporate minimum FTE enrollment objectives of (1) 5,000 students for doctoral-granting institutions, (2) 5,000 students for comprehensive colleges, (3) 1,000 students for liberal arts colleges, and (4) 2,000 students for two-year (community) colleges. We also recommended that state plans should, in general, incorporate maximum FTE enrollment objectives of (1) about 20,000 students for doctoral-granting institutions, (2) about 10,000 students for comprehensive colleges, (3) about 2,500 students for liberal arts colleges, and (4) about 5,000 students for two-year community colleges;[3] because first, no more savings in financial costs could be made beyond these levels, second, quality programs could be achieved certainly by these levels and, third, some disadvantages of size become more apparent after these limits are reached.

In addition, we recommended that, in developing their policies for state aid to private institutions, states should study and adopt policies providing financial incentives for expansion in those cases in which private institutions are clearly much too small for efficient operation, but that state policies should not be designed to force growth on private institutions of demonstrably high quality which are desirous of retaining unique characteristics associated with their comparatively small size. We also recommended that the federal government should encourage small institutions to grow by giving them priority in the awarding of construction grants and by aiding them through its "developing institutions" program.

Our suggested *minima* were based in part on economies of scale considerations and in part on the fact that very small institutions cannot offer an adequate curriculum to provide their students with both a broad general education background and an adequate choice of courses in specialized fields. We recognized quite explicitly that there were leading private universities, with heavy emphasis on rather specialized research programs, that might wish to retain

[3] These recommendations were presented in ibid., pp. 81–86.

some of the advantages of small size in relation to their particular objectives. We also recognized that there were leading liberal arts colleges with national reputations that might regard their relatively small size as contributing to a unique campus environment and that could count on their ability to attract students even if their tuition charges were relatively high and on their capacity to attract gifts from loyal alumni and other donors.

At the opposite end of the spectrum are many struggling private colleges that are caught in a vicious circle. They are heavily dependent on tuition as a source of income, and yet must be exceedingly cautious in raising tuition to meet rising costs because they are having severe enough difficulty in attracting students in the face of competition with low-cost public colleges. Where they are located in small communities in states characterized by out-migration, there may be no answer except merger with another appropriate institution—and abandonment of one of the two campuses involved. And there may be no answer for some of the financially squeezed small institutions except to close down, as some have done in recent years.

On the other hand, small colleges situated in promising locations may well be in a position to achieve reduced operating costs (in constant dollars) if somehow they can find the funds for the necessary capital expansion to achieve larger size—and, for those small colleges that do not have much capacity to attract alumni giving or foundation support, this is likely to mean that federal and/or state aid will be required to facilitate the necessary expansion. But, if that expansion *can* be achieved, the college may well find itself in a more viable position. Its preexpansion tuition may be somewhat below average costs (with other sources of funds perhaps barely making up or not quite making up the difference), but, because its marginal costs are likely to be below its average costs as it expands, it may be in a position to achieve a more favorable postexpansion relationship between tuition and average cost.

The current expansion of Williams College illustrates the advantages that can flow from expansion and also brings in another factor—that conversion of a single-sex institution to coeducation may provide special economies because of the fact that men and women tend to have differing patterns of choice of majors. However, it should be recognized that Williams approached its expansion from a position of relative financial strength, not weakness (15). In the spring of 1969 a special committee composed of administrators, faculty, and members of the Board of Trustees was appointed to explore the question of the desirability and feasibility of including women in the college. The committee recommended that Williams should enroll significant numbers of women students as regular members of the student body by 1971 and that the enrollment of women should be accomplished by expanding the total size of the college, not by reducing male enrollment. The committee examined carefully the economic implications of adding about 650 women to the existing undergraduate male student body of about 1,200 (on an FTE basis). It found that, apart from student aid expenses, the additional tuition and fees paid by 650 women would exceed the additional expenses on educational and general account by approximately $200,000 per year. This involved a projected marginal cost per student for the additional 650 students of slightly over $1,800, while tuition and fees per student in 1968–69 were $2,100. The average cost for the existing male student body for the same budget items (excluding sponsored research and certain special programs) was $4,350. These figures, the committee pointed out, compared quite closely with those given in the earlier report of Princeton's committee on the education of women at Princeton.

The Commission reiterates the recommendations that were made in its report, *New Students and New Places,* relating to the optimum size of institutions.

There is evidence, especially from studies conducted at the University of Toronto, that economies of scale in individual programs are more clearcut than in institutions as a whole (16, pp. 40–64).[4] This would be expected to be true particularly in universities, comprehensive colleges, and community colleges, where the influence of growing complexity as a factor offsetting economies of scale for the institution, as suggested above, is important. And, in graduate education, especially, a critical number of faculty members is needed in any given department if graduate education of high quality is to be provided. There is a tendency for high quality departments offering graduate work to be large departments, although the converse is not true—size does not guarantee quality (17, p. 99).

[4] Professor Richard W. Judy, Director, Systems Research Group, University of Toronto, made a statement to this effect at one of the conferences on effective use of resources sponsored by the Commission in November 1971.

These considerations lend added weight to the recommendations made later in this report urging caution in the adoption of new degree programs and stressing the need for periodic programmatic review with a view to eliminating degree programs that cannot be operated economically because they are generating very few degrees.

When a college or university launches a move toward more effective use of its resources, no step is more important than a careful analysis of costs, in relation not only to appropriate measures of input, such as FTE enrollment, but also in relation to appropriate measures of output or quality, such as credit hours completed, degrees awarded, performance of graduates on the Graduate Record Examination, and ratings of its departments in the studies of graduate education that have been conducted by the American Council on Education and other agencies.

Cost and output studies should include carefully compiled data on each department. Experience has indicated that, when a department chairman finds that costs per FTE enrollment or faculty-student ratios in his department are exceptionally high and that the difference cannot be explained fully, or perhaps even partly, on a satisfactory basis (such as high costs in science), he is likely to cooperate with the administration in efforts to bring these costs down. Furthermore, the department-by-department comparative analysis is likely to shed light on the reasons for excessively high costs in some departments—there may be a comparatively high ratio of support personnel to faculty, or a small average class size, or a heavy proliferation of courses, or a problem of waning student interest in the field.

In recent years, there has been a great deal of discussion and debate about how to develop appropriate measures of output and quality in higher education and about the possible application of Program and Planning Budget Systems (PPBS) to higher education. Much of this discussion has generated a certain amount of skepticism about the possibility of developing ideal measures of quality or benefits in higher education. Even such an authority on PPBS as President Charles J. Hitch of the University of California, who introduced this type of analysis in the United States Department of Defense in the early 1960s, has become dubious about its general utility in higher education, at least until a great deal more basic research has been undertaken. But there is general agreement on the need for an office of institutional research or its equivalent, especially in large institutions, and for a sustained effort to conduct cost-benefit analyses, even though there are difficulties involved in measuring benefits. There are also intricacies involved in measuring costs, because many costs in higher education are joint costs (joint costs of graduate and undergraduate education, joint use of library space by students in various fields, etc.). Despite these difficulties, the effort must be made. The problem has been well put by Alain Enthoven, who has also had experience with PPBS in the Department of Defense:

. . . I would not waste much time trying to develop an index of total knowledge, discovered or transmitted, in the hope that I could then use it to evaluate alternative programs. . . . Rather, I would begin by trying to understand very well where we are now, and on what basis allocation decisions are now being made, and what might be done to improve that basis. . . .

Because there is no agreement on purposes or on relative values, there is no "optimum" program for the university. There are only better and worse programs. Avoiding bad programs is a sufficiently ambitious goal to keep us all occupied for many years (18, pp. 52–53).

Comparative cost studies for groups of institutions can also be of great value in identifying cost differences that may not be entirely explained by differences in quality. One of the most illuminating of such recent studies was *The Twelve College Cost-Quality Study,* conducted by McKinsey and Company for 12 relatively prestigious colleges and universities in Pennsylvania (19). The study revealed wide differences in costs per student, particularly in sciences, as well as quite substantial differences in course enrollments per FTE faculty member. There were also wide variations in such items as administrative costs per student. The individual colleges are now studying these results, with a view, among other things, to identifying programs that have unusually high costs that may not be wholly explained by high quality.

One of the most interesting aspects of the findings related to the role of growing student aid expenditures in explaining growing deficits for these institutions. They had a combined deficit of $1.2 million in 1969–70, as compared with an operating surplus of $3.6 million in 1965–66.[5] But in 1970–71, the 11 institutions for which

[5] The report does not indicate the amount of the overall deficit in 1970–71.

McKinsey had earlier financial data reported student-aid deficits (excess of student aid expenditures over revenues specifically earmarked for student aid) of $4 million which was largely offset by surpluses from other accounts. The student aid deficit was projected to grow to $8 million by 1975–76. This finding, which is similar to the results of a number of other recent studies, lends strong support to the principle of relating federal aid to grants for low-income students and to cost-of-education supplements based on the number of student grant-holders enrolled by the institution, as recommended by the Commission.[6] Not only is the principle sound in terms of federal government responsibility for equality of opportunity and for all other reasons discussed in earlier reports, but it would relate institutional aid directly to a factor playing a major role in accounting for deficits, particularly in private institutions.[7]

All these considerations indicate the critical importance to every institution of higher education of a program of institutional research, a problem which is discussed more fully in Appendix B. In relatively large universities and colleges, there should be an office of institutional research or its equivalent. Relatively small institutions are likely to find it advantageous to unite with nearby similar institutions in a jointly sponsored program of institutional research. In fact, here is one function which would particularly lend itself to consortium arrangements, which would have the special advantage in this case of facilitating comparative cost analyses.

The Commission recommends that all relatively large institutions of higher education maintain an office of institutional research or its equivalent and that relatively small institutions seek to enter into arrangements with nearby similar institutions to conduct jointly sponsored programs of institutional research.

---

[6] See the Commission's reports, *Quality and Equality: New Levels of Federal Responsibility for Higher Education* (1968); *Quality and Equality: Revised Recommendations, New Levels of Federal Responsibility tor Higher Education* (1970); and *Institutional Aid: Federal Support to Colleges and Universities* (1972).

[7] At one time it was more or less taken for granted that a public institution of higher education could not incur a deficit, but an appreciable and growing number of public institutions have reported deficits in the last few years. Like private institutions, they can, for example, permit expenditures from endowment funds to exceed the income from those funds.

The Commission also recommends that all appropriate agencies—the U.S. Office of Education, the Southern Regional Education Board, the Western Interstate Commission on Higher Education, and similar bodies—give high priority to the development of more adequate data on the behavior of costs, income, and output in higher education.

4. Acceleration and Integration of Programs

The most promising single avenue toward more effective use of resources in higher education is provided by current and proposed changes in degree structures.[1]

1 Incorporation of the last year of high school into the first year of college

2 Incorporation of the first year in college into the last year of high school

3 A change to the three-year, rather than a four-year, bachelor of arts degree either through reducing requirements or through operating on a year-round basis

4 Credit given to students by examination for work accomplished outside the formal classroom

5 Integration of bachelor's and master's programs

6 Horizontal integration of overlapping or duplicating programs

7 Development of new types of master's programs that will provide more effective preparation for teaching in community colleges and, to some extent, in four-year colleges (e.g., the M. Phil. degree)

8 Placing greater emphasis on other two-year master's programs of a professional type, e.g., the Master in Human Biology degree, which would prepare an individual to be a physician's assistant, to teach at an appropriate level, or to go on for an M.D., D.D.S., or a Ph.D.

9 Emphasizing development of a four-year Doctor of Arts degree as the standard degree for college teachers and for many positions in government, industry, and academic administration

10 Reducing the length of time required to complete the work for the Ph.D. and the M.D. degrees

[1] Recommendations for such changes were made in the Commission's report, *Less Time, More Options* (1970).

Some attention is also being given to the desirability of awarding the Associate of Arts degree to all students successfully completing a lower-division program, whether in two-year or four-year colleges.

These changes are being considered not only because they will achieve economies—for institutions and for students—but particularly because they are desirable on educational grounds. It is increasingly recognized, for example, that many students enter college better prepared than was the case several decades ago, and that there is substantial overlapping between what is taught in the last two years of high school and in the first two years of college.[2]

Major steps are being taken toward acceleration of undergraduate education in the California State University and College system, with nearly 300,000 students enrolled in the fall of 1971. Chancellor Glenn S. Dumke proposed early in 1971, that the granting of degrees be based on actual, carefully measured academic achievement rather than the present accumulation of required credits, hours, semesters, and classes attended. This, he said, could shorten the four-year period normally required for a bachelor's degree by "one half to one full year or more for many, if not for most, students." Students would be given much greater responsibility for their own learning, "which could be largely or entirely independent study." His proposal also encompassed college credit for extension courses and emphasis on advanced (sophomore) placement of qualified students, but he cautioned that the suggested changes were so revolutionary that they should be tried out in pilot projects on several campuses before being implemented throughout the system as a whole (22).[3]

---

[2] According to Chancellor Ernest Boyer of the State University of New York, entering freshmen are scoring roughly one grade-year ahead of their counterparts of 20 years ago on standardized achievement tests (20). A recent survey indicated that high school teachers believed that 30 percent of what is taught in the first two years of college repeats what is taught in the last two years of high school, while college professors thought that 23 percent of what is taught in the last two years of high school is repeated in the first two years of college. Their responses were based on examination of sample outlines of courses (21). This means that 50 to 60 percent of one full year is duplicated.

[3] A step toward implementation has been taken at San Francisco State College, where incoming freshmen in the fall of 1971 were granted an opportunity for sophomore standing on the basis of their performance on five examinations, covering the humanities and social and natural sciences (23). It should be noted, however, that provisions for advanced placement and for credit by examination had existed at the State Colleges for some years. The chancellor's proposals appeared to be intended to bring about greatly increased emphasis on them.

In May 1971, it was announced that the Wisconsin State University system was also adopting a program under which students could earn certain credits toward degrees by passing examinations. The program was designed primarily to encourage the enrollment of adults and veterans (24). In July, Chancellor Ernest Boyer of the State University of New York system announced plans for a pilot three-year program, which he hoped could accommodate 15 percent of the freshmen entering in the fall of 1971.

Both St. Louis University and George Washington University have adopted optional three year B.A. programs for students with high academic standing. At St. Louis University, the three-year B.A. will require the same number of credit hours—120 to 130—as the traditional four-year program (25 and 26). Harvard, Princeton, and numerous other institutions are studying the possibility of accelerating undergraduate teaching.

Among liberal arts colleges, Ripon College and Stephens College have both recently announced adoption of optional three-year programs for the B.A. degree.[4] However, at Stephens, there was no reduction in the 124 credit hours required for the degree—students would simply have to carry heavier course loads to graduate in three years—and it was predicted that, for the time being, the majority of students would continue to attend for the traditional four years (28). At Ripon, the requirement for the three-year degree would be 112 credit hours, as compared with 120 hours for the four-year degree, while students enrolled in the three-year program would have to earn a cumulative grade-point average of 2.75, as compared with 2.00 for the four-year candidate, and would have to carry an average course load of 18 to 19 hours per semester rather than 15 to 16 hours (29).[5]

One of the most interesting and carefully analyzed recommendations relating to the three-year B.A. is included in the report prepared for the Princeton Commission on the Future of the College by Marvin Bressler (31). He recommended a three-year B.A. program with a limited option to pursue a fourth year of study, but he did not consider Princeton's existing semester system well adapted to adoption of a three-year undergraduate program. Instead

---

[4] McKendree College has had a three-year B.A. program for some time, while Webster College has also recently adopted one (27).

[5] At Colgate University, where a task force has been studying a number of proposed changes, a preliminary report suggested a somewhat negative view toward a three-year B.A. (30).

he suggested a trimester system consisting of a sequence of 11-week, 6-week, and 11-week terms. The academic year would thus be four weeks longer than at present so that over a three-year period the student would be exposed to 84 weeks of instruction, the equivalent of three and one-half years as measured by the current program. The six-week term would be intended primarily for short courses designed to contribute to the student's general education. His proposal also called for continued emphasis on senior independent work on a thesis or a special project.

In April 1972 a Yale faculty committee recommended that the academic year be extended to begin in early September and end in late June to allow students to get bachelor's degrees in three years (32). Also, early in 1972, three-year degree programs were announced at Northwestern University and Florida Atlantic University (33).[6]

At least two universities have adopted a somewhat different approach toward acceleration. In May 1971, Rutgers University announced a program for gifted high school seniors to enroll at its Newark College of Arts and Sciences on a full-time or part-time basis (34). Similarly, Lehigh University opened its classes to qualified high school students from the surrounding area, with a view to providing opportunities for advanced standing to those who ultimately enrolled in the university (35).

Still another approach to acceleration is exemplified by a proposal made at Johns Hopkins University and a program adopted at Bucknell University in the spring of 1971. President Milton Eisenhower of Johns Hopkins indicated that, to help make the university more attractive to transfer students, consideration was being given to establishing four-year programs leading to the master's degree and new accelerated programs leading to the Ph.D. An important element, he said, would be "to blur the distinction between undergraduate and graduate studies" (36). At Bucknell, students in biology will be able to earn both bachelor's and master's degrees in four years. Summer sessions for research and intensive courses will allow participants to receive a bachelor's degree in June of their senior year and a master's in August. Similar programs are planned by the chemistry and mechanical engineering departments (37).

---

[6] Florida Atlantic University is an upper-division institution. Its plan would allow high school graduates to get a degree in three years, with all work at the junior and senior level.

These recent developments suggest that colleges and universities are adopting a wide variety of approaches to acceleration of undergraduate education. Greater emphasis on opportunities for students to achieve advanced standing and to receive credit by examination are being emphasized by some institutions rather than a shift to a three-year curriculum. Thus far there appears to have been reluctance to reduce the number of credit hours required for the B.A. appreciably in those colleges and universities that have adopted an optional three-year program, but the Bressler proposals for Princeton are likely to be widely studied and perhaps will stimulate serious consideration of comprehensive curriculum changes in connection with adoption of a three-year B.A.

The trend toward acceleration of undergraduate education, whatever form it takes, will result in substantial economies for students — in direct educational costs and in reduction of the length of time during which earnings must be foregone. It will also result in economies for high schools (where seniors are encouraged to enroll in nearby colleges). The impact on institutional expenditures in higher education will be more complex. There will be significant savings in both operating expenses and capital costs for higher education as a whole because of a reduction in the number of students who are enrolled in their fourth year of undergraduate work. However, because attrition is high in American higher education, total enrollment of students in their fourth year of undergraduate education represents only 17 percent of total undergraduate enrollment (38, p. 25). The opportunity to graduate in three rather than four years would probably also induce some students who might have dropped out of a four-year program to stay on and complete the work for a three-year B.A. degree. Some students who entered higher education relatively poorly prepared, moreover, might require four years to complete the work for the degree. Thus we estimate that, if all institutions were to adopt a straightforward three-year B.A., there would be a reduction of only some 10 to 15 percent in total undergraduate enrollment and in institutional expenditures on undergraduates, as compared with the situation if the four-year B.A. were generally retained.

For individual institutions, there may be no saving in operating costs if the institution decides to increase the size of its entering class so as to spread over its three-year program (with due allowance for attrition) the number of students who formerly made up the fourth year class. The Bressler proposals for Princeton contemplate such an increase and the possibility of admitting more women to Princeton than had earlier been planned, without the need for incurring more capital costs for dormitories. This means that Princeton will, over a period of years, be able to increase the size of each of its classes without increasing the size of its faculty or incurring additional capital costs.

For higher education as a whole, the saving in capital costs will be relatively greater than the saving in operating costs. We estimate that about one-third of the capital costs that would have to be incurred in the 1970s to accommodate increased undergraduate enrollment could be saved if there were a general shift to a three-year B.A.

As we shall see at a later point, some colleges and universities are adopting plans which simultaneously reduce somewhat the length of time required for the B.A., provide for year-round operations, increase the size of the undergraduate student body (thereby achieving economies of scale), and provide for more flexible patterns of participation through deferred admissions and/or provision for terms spent away from the campus. We believe that such combinations of approaches to both academic reform and effective use of resources are likely to become increasingly common.[7]

Also underway on a substantial scale is a movement toward acceleration, as well as integration, of education in the health sciences.[8] This movement is being encouraged through the Comprehensive Health Manpower Act of 1971, which provided bonuses for acceleration in connection with federal capitation payments to medical and dental schools.

By the fall of 1971, it was reported that at least some students could graduate in three years at 21 medical schools.[9] Six other schools have programs which will graduate doctors six years after high school graduation by closely meshing premedical education in

---

[7] At the same time, it must be recognized that there are some small, underfinanced colleges, drawing their students from a limited local area, that will not benefit budgetwise from straightforward conversion to a three-year B.A. because they will not be able to attract students to replace the reduction associated with elimination of a fourth year and therefore will face a loss of tuition revenue as well as a less economical scale of operation.

[8] Recommendations for acceleration and integration of medical and dental education were made in the Commission's report, *Higher Education and the Nation's Health* (1970).

[9] A more recent report, in March 1972, indicated that 35 medical schools had adopted three-year programs (39).

their parent universities with their own programs, while several are providing opportunities for students to earn the M.D. degree five years after graduating from high school. One of the most interesting of these is at Jefferson University in Philadelphia, which has had a coordinated program with The Pennsylvania State University under which highly qualified students can receive both their B.S. and M.D. five years after high school. Students spend five quarters at the Penn State campus, and then three years at Jefferson, with summer school work back at Penn State following the second and third years at Jefferson (40).

A recent proposal for acceleration has come from a curriculum study committee of the Association of American Law Schools. Its report recommends, among other things:

1 Shortening by as much as two years the time from a student's freshman year in college until his graduation from law school. Only three years of undergraduate study would be required for admission to law school, and as little as two years in law school would be required for the J.D. degree.

2 Creation of a new Master of Arts in Law degree to be awarded after one year of graduate study

3 Creation of a major in law for undergraduates

4 Training students for new "allied legal professions" to provide counseling and advocacy services in such fields as family welfare, labor, and taxation law

However, the report was not submitted to the association for action — according to one of the committee members, "it would have been overwhelmingly defeated, with each person giving a different reason" (41).

The challenges facing graduate education are among the most difficult facing higher education today. As suggested later, we do not believe that the leading research universities should reduce the scope of their graduate programs, except perhaps on a highly selective, carefully planned, basis. There will always be a need for exceptionally able holders of doctor's degrees. But we do believe that in a rapidly worsening job market for Ph.D.'s, graduate education should aim at increased breadth in the training of Ph.D.'s who plan to go into college teaching and should place increased emphasis on the Doctor of Arts degree as the most appropriate type of preparation for those doctoral candidates who are aiming at careers that will involve primarily the teaching of undergraduates and training of candidates for the master's degree.

In an environment in which employment opportunities for faculty members will be increasing at a steadily declining rate, breadth and versatility will be advantageous for young holders of doctor's degrees planning to enter college teaching, although there will continue also to be some demand—though much less buoyant than in the 1960s—for young scholars with specialized research training for jobs in universities, government, and industry. But the Doctor of Arts degree—with its relatively greater emphasis on breadth—will be especially appropriate for the rising proportion of young job seekers who are likely to find themselves accepting positions in comprehensive colleges and community colleges.

The first D.A. program in the United States was established at Carnegie-Mellon University in 1967. Subsequently both the Council of Graduate Schools and the American Association of State Colleges and Universities issued guidelines for institutions interested in developing the new degree. In June 1970 the Carnegie Corporation of New York announced that it had awarded grants totaling $935,000 to 10 institutions to plan new graduate programs aimed at improving the quality of college teaching. "With one possible exception," it was announced, "the planning envisages that this will be the Doctor of Arts degree."[10]

By May 1971, the Council of Graduate Schools reported that five institutions had established D.A. degree programs, and that plans were being developed for establishment of D.A. programs at 26 other institutions (Appendix A, Table A-2).

In December 1971, the Council of Graduate Schools issued its *Supplemental Statement on the Doctor of Arts Degree, 1972.* Clearly by this time the Council was concerned about indications that the establishment of D.A. programs might lead to undesirable proliferation of doctoral-granting institutions. In its March 1970 statement it had said that "the new degree should be offered in well-established universities which already offer the Ph.D. in order that the Doctor of Arts may utilize the academic validity and reputation of graduate study in those universities, thus ensuring high standards and its acceptance in graduate education." In its December 1971 statement, the Council reaffirmed this position and went on to say:

---

[10] The recipients of the planning grants included Ball State University, Brown University, Claremont University Center, Dartmouth College, Idaho State University, Massachusetts Institute of Technology, University of Michigan, State University of New York at Albany, University of Washington, and Washington State University.

Distinguished graduate schools which have strong resources—reflected in regional and national reputations and which are accredited by recognized accrediting associations—presumably have necessary academic resources to offer the Doctor of Arts. However, the Doctor of Arts degree should not be automatically authorized by the Graduate Council or Faculty. . . .

The Doctor of Arts must be authorized only in fields with appropriate academic strength in the universities. The Council of Graduate Schools views as unacceptable automatic conversion of Doctorates of Education into Doctor of Arts degrees.

A major question involves adoption of the Doctor of Arts by institutions which have never offered doctoral study in any area or discipline; such universities are usually characterized as "emerging institutions." The Council of Graduate Schools views the proliferation of degree programs by less well-recognized institutions with serious concern. The Doctor of Arts must not be viewed as a less expensive version of the Ph.D. or as a means by which "emerging institutions can inexpensively offer doctoral study" (42, pp. 7–8).

We agree that the Doctor of Arts degree should be introduced into the leading research universities. Some other institutions, however, have both the interest and the capacity to introduce it as well, particularly within the category which we have called "comprehensive colleges and universities." New D.A. programs should be limited, however, to academic departments of high quality and of adequate size for economical operations.

We note that in most instances the latter stages of preparation for the D.A. will be less costly than the corresponding stages of preparation for the Ph.D. There will be less need for use of computers, expensive laboratories, and highly specialized library collections.

We are convinced that, by reducing the length of time involved, by reducing duplication of effort, and in other ways, the cost of graduate education can be reduced by the same 10 to 15 percent we have suggested as being possible for undergraduate education.

Probably exceeding the number of institutions that have adopted changes in degree structure in the last few years is the number of institutions that are making careful studies of possible changes. The Commission believes that the intensive review of degree structures that is underway holds great promise, not only for constructive economies in higher education, but also for the elimination of overlapping and duplication in the curricula at various levels of education, for a closer relationship between preprofessional and professional education, and for widening the range of options for students.

The Commission reiterates the recommendations made in its report, *Less Time, More Options,* for changes in degree structures.

One of the factors contributing to ineffective use of resources in higher education is the proliferation of degrees. According to Seymour Harris, from 1643 to a relatively recent year, American institutions of higher education had awarded 2,452 different degrees, and in this recent year were offering 1,600 degrees (43). One of the Commission's recommendations in *Less Time, More Options,* was that the total number of degrees awarded be reduced to about one-tenth of that number, to about 160. The process of pruning programs that is now going on in higher education is probably reducing the number of degrees offered in individual institutions, although it may not be reducing the overall number of degrees.

The Commission reiterates its recommendation for greatly reducing the number of different types of degrees awarded in higher education.

5. Retention Rates and the "Captive Audience"

Some commentators on effective use of resources in higher education place major emphasis on increasing retention rates. We agree that the resources of higher education are ineffectively utilized when students drop out because they have, let us say, been subjected to poor teaching. But we do not believe that colleges and universities should strive to hold the 5 to 15 percent or so of students who are there because of social pressures and are not really interested in continuing their education—the "captive audience."[1] Nor do we believe that efforts should be made to retain students who have been given ample opportunity but have shown that they cannot "make the grade" in higher education.

Our goal of "universal access" but not "universal attendance" has been expressed in *The Open-Door Colleges* (p. 15) and in other reports.[2]

The Commission believes that access to higher education should be expanded so that there will be an opportunity within the total system of higher education in each state for each high school graduate or otherwise qualified person. This does not mean that every young person should of necessity attend college—many will not want to attend, and there will be others who will not benefit sufficiently from attendance to justify their time and the expense involved. . . .

Within the system of higher education, the community colleges should follow an open-enrollment policy, whereas access to four-year institutions should generally be more selective.

---

[1] We estimate the size of the "captive audience" to be about 5 to 15 percent on the basis of various studies of student attitudes.

[2] The considerations involved were discussed at some length in the Commission's report, *A Chance to Learn* (1970).

Another way of stating the main point is that we believe students who may have been poorly motivated in high school or who may have received inferior education in ghetto schools should be given "a second chance," but that some of those who find that they cannot succeed in an academically oriented program may be successfully guided into an occupational program and into employment.

Nevertheless, we recognize that the dropout rate in American institutions of higher education is high. However, a recent study has indicated that dropout rates are lower than a number of earlier studies had implied (44). Although the dropout rate varies widely among types of institutions, this recent study concluded that nearly 70 percent of all students who enter four-year colleges as freshmen eventually receive a bachelor's degree, while nearly 55 percent of those entering two-year colleges receive an associate degree. The study was based on a follow-up survey of the 1966 entering freshman class four years later. And, if we examine results of studies of reasons for discontinuing, we find that substantial proportions of students discontinued under circumstances that might have been prevented—they dropped out for financial reasons or because they were "lonesome and unhappy" (45, p. 91). One dean on a large campus recently told of accidentally encountering a student who was filling out a withdrawal form. When he questioned the student, he was shown a list of the student's debts and an estimate of how much money he would need to finish the term. The student was withdrawing because he did not think he could borrow any more and simply did not have the funds to continue. The dean promptly arranged to provide him with enough student aid to complete the term.

It is commonplace to recommend the need for improved counseling as a means of increasing retention rates. But there is also a need for a practice that is frequently found in firms with progressive personnel policies but quite uncommon in higher education—the "exit interview." Such a practice would not only uncover preventable cases in which students drop out for financial reasons but would provide the institution with useful information about cases of ineffective teaching, indifferent or ineffective handling of student complaints, and the like.

The Commission recommends that institutions of higher education seek to increase their retention rates through improved counseling programs, where these are deficient, and through establishing the practice of conducting an "exit interview" with every student who plans to withdraw.

On the other hand, as much of the earlier discussion in this and other Commission reports suggests, we do not believe that students should be dissuaded from "stopping out" of higher education for a period. And we believe that colleges and universities should seek to reduce the "captive audience." One useful approach to this problem is through the admissions office. Admissions officers should attempt, through appropriate questioning, to identify students who are applying merely because of parental pressure or because "all their friends are going to college," and who might be better off in a job or in an occupational program or in a different type of college.[3]

As a means of identifying the dissatisfied students who are already there, it might be desirable to initiate a policy of an annual interview with all students. Admittedly this would be costly, but the costs might well be offset by savings associated with decisions of dissatisfied students to discontinue as a result of counseling in the annual interview. In large institutions, such programs might be initially tried out on a sampling or pilot basis, with a view to determining how effective they might be on a larger scale.

The number of reluctant attenders appears to be particularly high at the graduate level.

If, as we have recommended earlier, institutions widely adopted the practice of awarding the Associate in Arts degree after two years as an undergraduate and the Master of Philosophy degree after two years as a graduate student, convenient periods for reassessment would be created.

However, we believe that the main attack on this problem must be made long before the student enters college—through improved counseling in high school designed to identify students who may have the ability to enter college but who lack the motivation. Despite prolonged interest in educational circles in expanding and improving high school counseling programs, they continue to be weak or nonexistent in too many cases.

---

[3] A former Princeton admissions officer told of following a practice of attempting to identify able applicants whom he felt would probably be better off in a more vocationally oriented institution, and counseling them accordingly.

The Commission recommends that colleges and universities inaugurate programs designed to discourage poorly motivated students from entering and from continuing once they have entered. These programs should be designed to include appropriate counseling of applicants, generally through the admissions office, as well as counseling of all undergraduate students, perhaps through the medium of a regular annual interview.

We also recommend that high school counseling programs be strengthened and improved, not only for the purpose of guiding students to appropriate colleges or to appropriate jobs or occupational programs, but also to dissuade poorly motivated students from entering college.

6. Utilization
of Faculty Time

Salaries of faculty members represent a major item of expense in higher education, accounting, on the average, for about one-third of educational and general expenditures (less organized research), for about two-thirds of expenditures for instruction and departmental research, and for about 22 percent of total current-funds expenditures.[1] Furthermore, the size of the faculty tends to determine the need for other types of expenditures, such as those for support personnel, library volumes, computer expense, and office space.

1. STUDENT-FACULTY RATIOS

Achieving a significant increase in the student-faculty ratio is a major avenue to effective use of resources in a college or university, provided it can be accomplished without sacrificing quality. A low student-faculty ratio has traditionally been regarded as an indication of high quality and has been one of the desiderata sought by accrediting agencies. And yet, a number of studies have shown that there are wide variations in student-faculty ratios among institutions that are similar in type and, more strikingly, even among those that can on some reasonably objective basis be rated as similar in quality (46, 47, and 48). There are also wide variations from department to department within institutions.

This is not to suggest that there is no relationship between student-faculty ratios and quality. Radner' has shown that there is a strong and significant positive relationship among universities between ratios of faculty to students and quality, as measured by Cartter's study of quality in graduate education (13) and numbers

---

[1] These proportions vary by type of institution and tend to be smaller in universities than in other types of institutions (see Tables C-6, C-12, C-18, and C-19, Appendix C).

of Woodrow Wilson fellows entering each institution (holding constant other commonly used measures of quality such as faculty salaries and percentages of faculties with Ph.D. degrees). Moreover, the relationship is more strongly positive in private than in public universities (46).

However, to a large extent, the existing student-faculty ratios in most institutions are results of more or less unplanned historical evolution—a strong department chairman here, a decision to adopt a particular teaching method there, the impact of the adoption of an honors program, a decision in a leading research university to create a certain number of prestige professorships with minimal or no teaching responsibilities, or the availability of a special private gift or of public funds for a favored program such as agriculture. In view of this, it is highly unlikely that the overall student-faculty ratio in any given institution is optimal.[2]

An important consideration, however, is that during the greater part of the 1960s student-faculty ratios were rising in most types of institutions with no apparent adverse effect on quality (Table 8). Private universities constituted an exception between 1959 and 1963, but after that their ratios rose until they returned to about their 1955 level.[3] Exceptions to the rising trend in student-faculty ratios were the public two-year colleges, where student-faculty ratios have tended to change very little, and the private two-year colleges, where the ratios tended to decline somewhat from 1961 on. The history of generally rising student-faculty ratios in the 1960s cautions that savings from this source may have been significantly exhausted already. There are, however, a number of

---

[2] By optimal, we mean a student-faculty ratio which results from an appropriate mix of class sizes, a relatively equitable relationship among student-faculty ratios from department to department (allowing for differences in such factors as ratios of graduate enrollment to total enrollment), reasonable teaching loads, and other factors contributing to effective use of faculty resources. Clearly the optimal ratio for any given institution can only be approximately determined.

[3] The decline from the late 1950s to 1963 was associated with a pronounced increase in graduate enrollment as a percentage of total enrollment in private universities and is appreciably reduced when we convert the ratios to a weighted basis. Graduate enrollment was also rising rapidly in public universities during this period, but not as a percentage of total enrollment. According to William G. Bowen, the overall proportion of graduate students in all universities was almost exactly the same in the fall of 1963 (16.8 percent) as in the fall of 1955 (16.3 percent), but for private universities the proportion increased from 18.2 to 23.9 percent during this period (49, p. 12).

TABLE 8   Ratios of full-time equivalent students to full-time equivalent faculty members, by type and control of institution, United States, 1955 to 1967

	Four-year institutions						Two-year institutions		
	Public			Private					
Year	Universities	Other four-year	Total	Universities	Other four-year	Total	Public	Private	Total
				Unweighted					
1955	13.0	15.3	13.8	11.1	12.7	12.0	22.5	15.2	20.6
1957	12.0	15.0	13.1	10.5	12.7	11.8	20.5	15.3	19.2
1959	12.9	15.9	14.1	10.4	12.9	11.8	20.7	17.2	19.9
1961	13.6	17.1	15.0	10.0	13.6	12.0	20.6	18.5	20.2
1963	14.4	17.2	15.5	9.5	13.5	11.8	21.1	18.3	20.6
1966	15.9	17.4	16.5	10.9	14.2	12.9	21.0	17.1	20.4
1967	15.7	17.9	16.6	11.3	14.3	13.1	20.3	17.2	19.9
				*Weighted**					
1955	15.4	16.5	15.8	14.2	13.5	13.8	22.5	15.2	20.6
1957	14.4	16.1	15.0	13.7	13.4	13.5	20.5	15.3	19.2
1959	15.9	17.3	16.4	13.9	13.7	13.8	20.7	17.2	19.9
1961	16.9	18.6	17.6	13.5	14.5	14.0	20.6	18.5	20.2
1963	17.8	19.0	18.3	13.2	14.5	13.9	21.1	18.3	20.6
1966	20.1	19.5	19.8	15.7	15.5	15.5	21.0	17.1	20.4
1967	20.1	20.2	20.2	16.2	15.6	15.9	20.3	17.2	19.9

* Weighted ratios are derived by using the formula U + 3G/F, where U = FTE undergraduate enrollment, G = FTE graduate enrollment, and F = FTE senior faculty. The weighting of graduate enrollment on a 3 to 1 basis reflects estimates of the relative cost per FTE student of graduate and undergraduate education that have been made at various universities. "Senior" faculty members are defined as all teachers above the level of teaching assistants.

SOURCE: Adapted from U.S. Office of Education data by Gus W. Haggstrom of the University of California, Berkeley.

ways in which better utilization of faculty members can still be obtained in most institutions.

2. THE SIZE OF CLASSES   Traditionally, small classes have been regarded as providing a superior learning environment. Yet research on the impact of class size on learning has failed to reveal a clearly significant relationship between class size and student achievement.

W. J. McKeachie and his associates in psychology at the University of Michigan have conducted research on teaching effectiveness for many years. Their recent review of the results of such research by themselves and others since the 1920s has been summarized as follows:

1   When scores on class quizzes and examinations were used as the index of learning, neither large classes nor small classes were found to be clearly superior to the other.

2   When retention of knowledge for one to two years was the measure of learning, the small class was found slightly superior.

3   When problem-solving or changes in attitude were the index of learning, the small class was found to be superior (50, p. III-20).

Among other long-time students of higher education, Alvin Eurich has concluded that "class size seems to be a relatively minor factor in educational efficiency, measured in terms of student achievement," and Lewis Mayhew has commented that "The blunt fact is that class size has very little relationship to student achievement" (ibid.).

The late Beardsley Ruml proposed doing away with medium-sized classes and concentrating on large lectures and small seminars (51). More recently, Bowen and Douglass have examined Ruml's proposal and several other proposals for changes in modes of instruction and have developed their own "eclectic plan," which would include: "(1) a few large lecture courses common to all or most students; (2) courses calling for programmed independent study either with or without learning stations and mechanical systems as in the Kieffer plan; (3) courses with emphasis on tutorials; and (4) 'conventional classes'" (52, p. 73). In their judgment "good education calls for a mixture of various methods so that students can have varied experiences as they pursue their college careers and so that professors can teach in the manner that suits their talents and taste" (ibid.). They estimated that in a liberal arts college with 1,200 students and a student course load of eight courses per year the average cost per student per course would be $134 under their eclectic plan, as compared with $208 to $285 under more conventional plans of instruction, depending on the average teaching load.

The Bressler Report, cited earlier, recommended a carefully planned mixture of undergraduate class sizes at Princeton, ranging from one student in senior tutorials to 170 in freshman "exploration" lectures (31).

For a variety of reasons, independent study is receiving increased emphasis in programs for academic reform and in experimental colleges.[4] Independent study courses encourage flexibility and variety, and can be tailored to the student's individual interests. They also facilitate the dropping of course offerings that are attracting too few students. There is a strong case for a policy under which classes where fewer than a stipulated minimum number of students registered in a given term will be dropped—either for that term or permanently, depending on the history of registration in the course. The California Coordinating Council on Higher Education recently conducted a survey of policies regarding class size in public institutions of higher education in other states and found that only 20 of the 46 respondent institutions had a written policy. The majority of universities with written policies set lower minima for graduate than for undergraduate classes, while six universities also set lower minima for upper-division than for lower-division classes. The range of minimum class sizes varied widely— from a minimum of two to a minimum of eight for graduate courses, and from a minimum of 10 to a minimum of 20 for lower-division classes (50, p. III-11).

3. THE PROLIFERATION OF COURSES Closely related to the question of class size is the problem of proliferation of courses. As one writer recently commented:

Few would argue that our colleges and universities are models of efficiency. Examples of apparent inefficiencies are not difficult to find. Perhaps the most obvious and also enduring example is the continuing proliferation of courses. In 1957 the Presidents' Committee on Education Beyond the High School, concerned with the proliferation of courses, urged that all faculties "earnestly and periodically review their own curricula in the light of the students' educational needs, major objectives and institutional resources." . . . Seven years later, Lewis B. Mayhew reviewed the same problem and suggested the situation was becoming more acute as institutions added more and more departments covering narrow areas of a discipline (10, p. 124).

[4] A recent article described the programs of two liberal arts colleges—experimental Hampshire College in Massachusetts and long established La Verne College in California—which are building their programs very largely around independent study (53). A Hampshire student progresses from one level to the next by taking an examination in each of Hampshire's three schools—humanities, social sciences, and natural sciences. He takes the exam when he feels ready for it and may receive credit by examination without having prepared for it through formal study at Hampshire.

As Seymour Harris has shown, the increase in the number of courses has been in large part, but not wholly, associated with the growth of graduate education (43). In part, also, the proliferation has been associated with the steady advancement of knowledge into new and more specialized areas. But institutions should be prepared to drop courses in which interest has been lagging when they decide to add new courses in subjects in which interest is growing.

There is an acute need for policies requiring regular review, not only of proposals for new courses, but also of existing course offerings, where such policies are not in effect. Individual departments or schools are sometimes prone to give in to the desire of a particular faculty member to give a course in a specialized aspect of his discipline simply to suit his own interests.

Professional associations could make a more significant contribution to the solution of this problem than they have been inclined to do by setting up committees to develop guidelines for appropriate undergraduate and graduate curricula in their disciplines. These should not be rigid or inflexible, but they could provide standards against which collegewide committees could judge the course offerings of individual departments. Visiting committees in individual subject fields could also play a role in suggesting the elimination of superfluous courses. Some universities follow a regular policy of appointing such visiting committees to assess the quality of departments or schools. The committees are typically composed of prestigious faculty members in the relevant discipline from other institutions. However, they seldom seem to concern themselves with such questions as proliferation of courses. The Commission believes that such policies should become more prevalent, primarily for the purpose of obtaining relatively independent assessments of quality, but coincidentally to bring about greater emphasis on overcoming problems of proliferation of courses.

4. TEACHING LOADS   Faculty teaching loads have become a matter of great controversy in the last few years, and in several states legislation has been enacted setting minimum weekly classroom contact hours for faculty members in public universities and colleges. But faculty teaching loads are also a matter of much misunderstanding on the part of legislatures and the general public.

When the "man on the street" hears that the average weekly teaching load at public University X is 6 hours per week, he is likely to conclude, not altogether surprisingly, that faculty members lead a "soft life" at the expense of the taxpayer. Even if he is a college graduate, he is likely to have little realization of the fact that preparation for class often consumes many more hours than a faculty member spends in the classroom, especially in graduate courses. He is also unlikely to have much conception of the time faculty members spend holding student office hours, supervising doctoral theses, conducting oral examinations of graduate students, and serving on departmental and campuswide committees. Nor does he have much understanding of the relationship between teaching and research, especially in graduate education.

In evaluating variations among institutions, it must be kept in mind that the chief impact of the enormous increase in enrollment of graduate students has been on the universities. Faculty members involved in graduate instruction cannot carry course loads as heavy as those carried by faculty members in exclusively undergraduate institutions if they are to devote adequate time to supervising Ph.D. theses, sitting on oral examination boards, and performing other time-consuming responsibilities associated with graduate education.

Faculty teaching loads have, however, declined appreciably in recent decades. Between 1931–32, when the U.S. Office of Education conducted a survey, and 1969, when the Carnegie Commission Survey of Students and Faculty Members was conducted, teaching loads declined considerably, especially in universities:

Median clock hours per week, 1931–32 and median classroom hours, 1969 of faculty members, by type and control of institution	1931–32		1969	
	Public	*Private*	*Public*	*Private*
*Research universities I**			6.0	5.2
Other doctoral-granting universities	15.0–15.3	14.4–15.8†	7.3	8.2
Comprehensive universities and colleges‡	16.7		11.0	10.0
Liberal arts colleges	†	†	11.2	11.0
Two-year colleges	17.8–18.2	17.0–18.0	15.1	13.6

* Includes only research universities classified in category 1.1 of the Carnegie Commission Classification of Institutions of Higher Education, as described in Appendix A of the Commission's report, *New Students and New Places* (1971).

† There was no category, "public liberal arts colleges," in the earlier survey, and private liberal arts colleges were grouped with private universities.

‡ There was no category, "comprehensive universities and colleges," in the earlier survey. We have used the data for teachers' colleges and normal schools, which were the predecessors of many of the comprehensive universities and colleges of today.

SOURCE: U.S. Office of Education, *National Survey of the Education of Teachers,* Bulletin No. 10, Washington, 1933, p. 182; and Carnegie Commission Survey of Students and Faculty, 1969.

Both sets of data indicate that formal teaching loads have tended to be lower in private than in public institutions. The only exception is "other doctoral-granting institutions." It should also be noted that the medians conceal rather wide variations in teaching loads in 1969, as shown in Table A-3, Appendix A.

With the rapid increase in graduate enrollment in the last few decades, there has also been, as might have been expected, a marked increase in the number of teaching assistants and other junior instructors in higher education. Thus the question naturally arises as to whether the decline in teaching loads of senior faculty (instructors and above) to which both the 1931–32 and 1969 data refer may have been at least partially offset by relatively increased use of teaching assistants. The answer is that there has been quite a pronounced increase in the ratio of junior instructors to senior faculty in public universities but not in other groups of institutions —in fact the ratio has declined in four-year colleges:

Ratios of junior instructors to senior faculty (instructors and above) in universities and other four-year institutions of higher education, public and private, selected years, 1955 to 1967–68

	Universities		Other four-year institutions	
	Public	Private	Public	Private
1955	0.13	0.20	0.08	0.06
1959–60	0.16	0.21	0.06	0.06
1967–68	0.21	0.20	0.06	0.04

SOURCE: Adapted from U.S. Office of Education data by Gus W. Haggstrom, University of California, Berkeley. Data for two-year colleges are not included because junior instructors are infrequently employed there.

In recent years there have been many surveys at individual institutions of higher education, usually based on questionnaires addressed to faculty members, designed to determine how many hours a week faculty members actually work and how they distribute their time among various aspects of their work. A study conducted by the National Academy of Sciences covering the period from 1940 to 1963 indicated that scientists employed in academic institutions consistently worked about 5 hours more per week than did scientists in nonacademic jobs (50, p. 6). A recent review of over 100 studies at institutions throughout the country indicated that faculty members on the average work more than 50 hours a week, but it was also pointed out that, because of differences in definitions of components of the work load and other methodological differences, the data on components were not comparable (54, p. 71).

Bowen and Douglass have adjusted results of recent surveys conducted at the Claremont Colleges and at the University of California so that they are reasonably comparable:

Allocation of faculty workweek, by average number of hours spent on each type of activity	Undergraduate faculties, Claremont Colleges		All faculties, University of California	
	Hours	Percent	Hours	Percent
All activities	55	100	60	100§
Instruction*	33	60	30	50
Administrative activities†	5	9	7	12
Research activities	12	22	19	32
Other activities‡	5	9	4	7

* Includes preparation for class, seeing students in class and out, and evaluating students' work.

† Includes service on faculty committees.

‡ Includes faculty involvement in "student affairs" and public service.

§ Items add to more than 100 because of rounding.

SOURCE: H. R. Bowen and G. K. Douglass: *Efficiency in Liberal Education: A Study of Comparative Instructional Costs for Different Ways of Organizing Teaching-Learning in a Liberal Arts College*, McGraw-Hill Book Company, New York, 1971.

The chief differences between the two sets of data are the longer workweek reported by University of California faculty members and, not unexpectedly, the fact that they spend more hours on research.

Some observers are skeptical about the results of such surveys, pointing out that the standards used by individual faculty members in distinguishing between "work" and other activities may vary considerably. This difficulty could be at least partially overcome if mailed questionnaires were supplemented by personal interviews with representative samples of faculty members. In any case, in an environment in which many questions are raised about how faculty members spend their time, it is useful for colleges and universities to develop carefully compiled data of this type in an attempt not only to encourage a more sophisticated understanding on the part of legislators and the general public, but also as a means of identifying inequities and cases in which teaching loads may be unduly light.

There are indications that teaching loads have increased, at least in some institutions, under the impact of financial stringency in the last few years. The Commission on Effective Use of Resources at

New York University, for example, reported in September 1969 that the largest dollar saving in the 1970–71 budget resulted from the guidelines established for faculty salaries and workloads. Faculty salaries were increased, but the increases were to be contingent on each school's ability to implement several types of instructional economies, including modest increases in teaching loads (55).

State legislation affecting teaching loads has recently been enacted in Florida, Michigan, Ohio, and Washington. In Michigan, the legislation called for minimum weekly classroom-contact hours of 10 a week in universities, 12 a week in other four-year colleges, and 15 a week in junior colleges (56). However, a year later a state court ruled that the legislation relating to hours of work, along with certain other restrictive provisions affecting Michigan's three state universities—the University of Michigan, Michigan State, and Wayne State—violated guarantees of autonomy for the universities in the state constitution (57). The Florida law specified that full-time faculty members must spend a minimum of 12 hours per week in the classroom, but administrators were given some flexibility so that nonteaching duties could be substituted in certain cases. In Washington, the legislature called for a 5 percent increase between 1970–71 and 1972–73 in the average weekly classroom hours of faculty members. New York's legislature passed a bill very similar to the Michigan legislation, but it was vetoed by the governor.

But teaching loads are a matter of concern in private, as well as in public institutions of higher education. We believe that the best way for colleges and universities to confront the problem of appropriate teaching loads is to involve the faculty itself in an analysis of the question and of the way in which it relates to current financial stringency, both in public and private universities. On the basis of extensive acquaintance with faculty members in various types of colleges and universities, we believe that most faculty members work long hours. Moreover, faculty members are in the best position to know which of their colleagues may be an exception to this generalization.

The American Association of University Professors has recently spoken out against legislatively mandated workloads. We share its opposition. The AAUP has also developed its own suggested workload standards. The Association noted that it favored full faculty participation in determining workloads and suggested as the "preferable pattern" 9 classroom hours a week for undergraduate instruction and 6 hours a week for instruction at least partly at the graduate level. Maximum workloads should be 12 hours at the undergraduate level and 9 hours at the graduate level. The major portion of the AAUP's *Statement on Faculty Workload* is reproduced in Appendix D.

5. RESEARCH AND PUBLIC SERVICE Research and public service have long been highly regarded functions of universities, and, to some extent, of other institutions of higher education as well. In this country, we have relied very heavily on universities for both basic research and some applied research — in contrast with the situation in many European countries in which research is largely conducted in government-supported institutes outside the universities. We believe that the marriage of higher education and research as it has developed in this country has produced, in general, demonstrably superior results. In some European countries, university teaching suffers, because the best minds — and often those most involved in advancing the frontiers of knowledge — are in research institutes divorced from universities. Contrariwise, research may suffer in some cases, because it does not become subjected to the questions of able students who, in this country, frequently uncover areas of weakness in the "conventional wisdom" or help to open up new lines of research inquiry.

However, research is predominantly a national concern. For the most part, the benefits of research ignore state boundaries. Thus, we cannot quarrel with the tendency of state legislatures in recent decades to regard financial support of research as predominantly a responsibility of the federal government and of private foundations. But we also cannot agree with the scornful attitudes toward faculty research activities that are sometimes displayed. The preeminence of the United States in the advancement of knowledge and technology is inextricably associated with the high quality of research in its leading research universities. And the use of reasonable portions of university faculty members' time on research should be regarded as desirable. The training of graduate students in research techniques is often intimately involved. Abuses, however, do occur when a faculty member becomes so involved in his own research as to be inaccessible to students.

It has occasionally been suggested that productivity in higher education could be increased if there were a more clearcut division of labor between teachers, researchers, and administrators. Those who are particularly gifted at teaching should teach, those who are productive researchers should confine their time to research, and those who are skilled as administrators should be engaged exclusively in administration (43). We cannot agree with this as a general principle. It is true that there are some productive researchers who are poor teachers, and some excellent teachers who are either uninterested in research or not very good at it. But we believe that in many cases scholars who are actively engaged in research are stimulating teachers and that, particularly at the advanced graduate level, it is exceedingly important for students to receive at least part of their training from professors who are actively engaged in advancing the frontiers of knowledge in their fields. These considerations are, of course, particularly relevant in universities.

The Carnegie Commission Survey of Students and Faculty provides evidence that the satisfaction of undergraduates with their college is not, in general, adversely affected by involvement of faculty members in research. In terms of overall evaluation of the student's institution, the percentage of undergraduates who responded that they were very satisfied or satisfied was higher (77 percent) in Research Universities I—universities with heavy emphasis on research—than in any of the other groups of institutions as classified by the Commission.[5] However, Research Universities II (72 percent) and Liberal Arts Colleges I (72 percent) ranked almost as well as Research Universities I in terms of overall undergraduate satisfaction. Nevertheless, when students were asked to mention specific aspects of their institution with which they were dissatisfied or very dissatisfied, the percentage mentioning "quality of classroom instruction" as a source of dissatisfaction was somewhat higher in Research Universities I (31 percent) and Research Universities II (31 percent) than in Liberal Arts Colleges I (25 percent) and Two-year Colleges (27 percent). The research universities were on a par with Liberal Arts Colleges II (31 percent) and came out considerably ahead of both doctoral-granting universities with less emphasis on research and comprehensive universities and colleges, in which substantially larger proportions of undergraduates expressed dissatisfaction with the quality of instruction.

American colleges and universities—especially the land-grant

---

[5] The students were responding to the question "What is your overall evaluation of your college? Very satisfied; satisfied; on the fence; dissatisfied; very dissatisfied."

universities—have a long tradition of public service as well as of research. The most conspicuous and formalized of these activities are found in extension divisions, teaching hospitals, and the like, but the more informal involvement of faculty members in various advisory capacities to federal, state, and local governments throughout the country is at least equally important. At the federal and state levels these advisory activities are usually financially compensated, but at the local level they often are not. Faculty members can, and frequently do, make distinctive contributions as members of city councils, boards of education, and local advisory committees on such problems as urban planning and taxation, with little or no monetary compensation.

6. CONSULTING ACTIVITIES Closely related to the controversy over teaching loads is another issue, the consulting activities of faculty members. There is little question that there are cases in which faculty members engage in outside consulting activities at the expense of adequate devotion of time to their teaching and other academic responsibilities, but it is also true that in many fields a moderate amount of consulting activity on the part of faculty members not only enables them to provide valuable public and private services, but also makes them much more interesting and productive teachers. The economist who serves on an advisory committee to the United States Treasury or the Council of Economic Advisers is often in a position to keep in particularly close touch with the development of national economic policy and, in turn, can involve his students in highly informed discussion and debate over the issues. An industrial relations specialist who serves as an arbitrator gains an understanding of collective bargaining at close range that cannot be gained in the library. A professor of architecture who is associated with an architectural firm or serves as a consultant to public or private bodies is constantly in a position to involve his students in the solution of actual problems. Similarly opportunities arise in the sciences, law, engineering, and other fields.

Although the Carnegie Commission Survey of Students and Faculty indicated that well over half of all faculty members were involved in consulting, with or without compensation, the proportion of time in a normal week devoted to this type of activity was, for the most part, very small (Table 9). There was some tendency for faculty members in private institutions to devote somewhat higher percentages of time to consulting activities than those in

TABLE 9 *Percentage of time in a normal work week devoted by faculty members to consulting activities, with or without compensation, by type and control of institution*

Percentage of time	Research universities I and II	Other doctoral-granting universities	Comprehensive universities and colleges	Liberal arts colleges*	Two-year colleges
			Type of institution		
			Public		
0	40.3	42.1	36.8		44.5
1 to 10	43.6	42.0	43.1		35.8
11 to 20	11.7	11.5	11.9		13.5
21 to 40	3.2	3.6	5.2		3.8
41 and over	1.2	0.8	3.0		2.4
Total percent	100.0	100.0	100.0		100.0
Percent with 11 hours or more of consulting activity	16.1	15.9	20.1		19.7
			Private		
0	34.3	44.6	39.4	40.3	34.7
1 to 10	43.0	37.0	38.9	38.2	38.8
11 to 20	15.6	12.4	14.8	16.1	25.7
21 to 40	4.7	4.6	3.7	3.6	0.8
41 and over	2.4	1.4	3.2	1.8	0.0
Total percent	100.0	100.0	100.0	100.0	100.0
Percent with 11 hours or more of consulting activity	22.7	18.4	21.7	21.5	26.5

*We have omitted data for public liberal arts colleges, because the number of respondents in this group was small.
SOURCE: Carnegie Commission Survey of Students and Faculty, 1969.

public institutions, and the smallest percentages of faculty members reporting 11 or more percent of their time spent on consulting activity were found in public universities.

Patterns of paid consulting activities varied significantly among groups of institutions (Tables A-4 and A-5, Appendix A). Except for the fact that relatively more faculty members in public than in private research universities reported no paid consulting activity, the patterns of differences among types of institutions were very similar for public and private institutions. However, there were interesting differences by types of employer or agency for which the consulting was done. Not surprisingly, faculty members in universities, especially private research universities, were more likely to report serving as paid consultants to federal and foreign government agencies, national corporations, nonprofit foundations, and research projects than faculty members in other types of institutions. Differences were, for the most part, less pronounced with respect to consulting for local business, government and schools.

The proportions of faculty members devoting 21 percent or more of their time to consulting in a normal work week were small but not insignificant. In the great majority of these cases, the proportion of time devoted was less than 40 percent. The results of the survey suggest that setting a general standard under which faculty members would be expected not to devote more than one day a week, on the average, to consulting activities—a policy currently followed in some institutions—would not affect many faculty members and would tend to reach the cases of abuse. The problem of enforcing such a standard is, of course, another matter. Deans and department chairmen should be expected to watch for cases of abuse. In some cases, faculty members in public institutions may be spending relatively large amounts of time in public service to state coordinating councils or other bodies where their work is directly germane to higher education.

Some medical schools urge faculty members to donate a portion of the income they receive from private practice to scholarship funds.

Actually, consulting activity is not the major source of supplemental faculty income. By far the largest source of supplemental income, especially in four-year colleges, is summer teaching (Table 10). Consulting activity is relatively important as a source of outside income only in universities. This is also true of compensation for research, which tends to be received chiefly in the summer.

Summer teaching is somewhat less important, relatively, as a source of income in private rather than in public institutions, whereas private practice—undoubtedly primarily by faculty members in such professional fields as medicine, law, engineering, and architecture—is relatively more important in private institutions.

Roughly half or more of faculty members in most types of institutions reported either no supplemental earnings or supplemental earnings of less than 10 percent (Table 11). However, the percentages reporting supplemental earnings of 20 percent or more were appreciable, especially in universities. And in private research

TABLE 10 *Largest source of supplemental earnings of faculty members, by type and control of institution*

Largest source of supplemental earnings	Type of institution				
	Research universities	Other doctoral-granting universities	Comprehensive universities and colleges	Liberal arts colleges*	Two-year colleges
Public					
Summer teaching	29.6	38.1	52.0		36.8
Teaching elsewhere (extension, etc.) other than summer teaching	3.4	4.4	5.7		23.1
Consulting	18.8	17.4	6.9		4.5
Private practice	6.0	6.1	6.9		7.2
Royalties (from publications, patents)	6.1	3.7	2.5		0.9
Fees for speeches and lectures	4.5	2.6	3.0		
Research salaries and payments	14.1	11.9	5.2		1.8
Other	17.5	15.8	17.8		25.7
Total percent	100.0	100.0	100.0		100.0
Private					
Summer teaching	14.3	28.5	40.5	38.7	37.4
Teaching elsewhere (extension, etc.) other than summer teaching	4.8	8.7	7.5	6.5	4.5
Consulting	22.0	19.9	9.8	8.1	7.8
Private practice	14.1	8.9	5.5	4.2	13.1
Royalties (from publications, patents)	9.6	2.1	1.6	4.1	
Fees for speeches and lectures	6.3	1.1	6.3	5.9	
Research salaries and payments	16.9	12.7	3.6	5.9	10.7
Other	12.0	18.1	25.2	26.6	26.5
Total percent	100.0	100.0	100.0	100.0	100.0

* We have omitted data for public liberal arts colleges, because the number of respondents in this group was small.

SOURCE: Carnegie Commission Survey of Students and Faculty, 1969.

TABLE 11 *Earnings above basic salary as a percentage of basic salary of faculty members, by type
and control of institution*

Earnings above basic salary as a percentage of basic salary	Research universities	Doctoral-granting universities	Comprehensive universities and colleges	Liberal arts colleges*	Two-year colleges
			Public		
0	19.6	17.4	24.4		16.6
1–9	30.2	28.5	32.5		38.1
10–19	21.1	22.8	24.6		20.7
20–29	15.5	14.8	10.0		14.8
30–39	6.0	8.9	3.5		3.6
40–49	2.4	2.4	1.4		1.1
50 and over	5.2	5.2	3.6		5.1
Total percent	100.0	100.0	100.0		100.0
Percent reporting 20 percent or more above basic salary	29.1	31.3	18.5		24.6
			Private		
0	13.5	20.1	18.9	29.1	27.0
1–9	26.3	27.0	28.4	36.9	41.3
10–19	18.6	21.1	28.4	21.4	16.8
20–29	14.4	17.3	10.1	7.3	2.8
30–39	6.0	3.5	5.0	1.5	8.1
40–49	3.8	3.6	1.8	1.8	0.8
50 and over	17.2	7.4	7.4	3.0	3.2
Total percent	100.0	100.0	100.0	100.0	100.0
Percent reporting 20 percent or more above basic salary	41.4	31.8	24.3	13.6	14.9

* We have omitted data for public liberal arts colleges, because the number of respondents in this group was small.
SOURCE: Carnegie Commission Survey of Students and Faculty, 1969.

universities the proportion reporting supplemental earnings of 20 percent or more was particularly high, while 17 percent reported supplemental earnings of 50 percent or more. This was probably related to the sizable proportion in this group who reported earnings from private practice. In some cases, the explanation of high outside earnings is a best-selling textbook.

7. LEAVES OF ABSENCE The tradition of the sabbatical, or seventh year off, usually with one-half pay—sometimes with two-thirds—is an old one in higher education. In many cases, faculty members prefer to take a semester off following 3 1/2 years of service, and the quarter system is introducing new patterns of short sabbaticals. In the Commission's judgment, sabbatical arrangements should not be greatly disturbed.

Acute financial stringency may require temporary suspension of sabbaticals, as was recently provided under legislation enacted in New York State, but we do not believe curtailing sabbatical arrangements, except where they may be unusually generous, is in the long-run interest of institutions of higher education. Princeton's Priorities Committee found, in its analysis of potential savings in the 1971–72 budget, that the university had an exceptionally generous leave of absence program—probably the most expensive program of its kind relative to the size of the institution. One of the Committee's recommendations, therefore, was to guarantee a paid leave of absence of one term to an assistant professor only during his first three-year appointment, but to drop the guarantee for his second three-year appointment (58).[6]

Often sabbatical privileges are limited to tenured professors or are less liberal for assistant professors than for those in higher ranks. We believe that assistant professors should have the same sabbatical rights as associate and full professors, especially under the conditions that will prevail in the late 1970s and in the 1980s. Promotional opportunities for assistant professors will be extremely limited, and they will need maximum encouragement in the development of their scholarly abilities.

A somewhat different problem is presented by leaves of absence to serve as a visiting professor elsewhere, to accept a temporary appointment in a government agency, or to work on a special project abroad. Opportunities for such appointments, especially for prestigious professors in leading universities, have been frequent in the last several decades. Institutions tend to have policies limiting the length of a continuous leave of absence to two or three years, but often there is no policy restricting the frequency with which faculty members may take leaves of lesser duration, and some faculty members have been away from their campuses almost as

---

[6] However, assistant professors on second three-year appointments would continue to be eligible for bicentennial preceptorships and would also be eligible to compete for the regular leaves of absence available formerly only to tenured faculty.

much as they have been there. When this happens it does not achieve effective use of resources. To be sure, the institution may be able to employ a substitute visiting professor at a lower rate of pay than that of the faculty member who is on leave, or parcel out his teaching responsibilities among younger and lower-paid faculty, but the chief objective of hiring the prestigious and high-priced individual in the first place—that of contributing to a stimulating intellectual environment for his students and his colleagues—is not being achieved. Probably the chief sufferers in these cases are graduate students at the doctoral-thesis stage.

8. SUPPORT PERSONNEL Faculty members should not be expected to spend their time on functions that can be carried out by administrative assistants, secretaries, properly supervised examination graders, and other support personnel. Across-the-board cutbacks affecting such personnel are not a desirable way of meeting financial stringency, although careful analysis may reveal some departmental or administrative offices that have managed over the years to acquire an unusually generous allotment of such personnel. As Balderston has shown, salaries of administrative and support personnel at the University of California tended to rise more rapidly than faculty salaries in the 1960s (59, p. 72), but as long as the levels of the former types of salaries are well below faculty salary levels, it will pay to substitute other kinds of labor for faculty labor wherever feasible.

When more support personnel is provided, then it is reasonable that faculty teaching loads might be increased; for example, a department chairman given a full-time "departmental administrative officer" might well be expected to teach more than before he received such assistance.

9. A SUMMING UP Achieving effective use of faculty time is central to a program aimed at effective use of resources in higher education. Clearly, colleges and universities with low student-faculty ratios need to give more attention to measures aimed at increasing these ratios and thus achieving more effective use of their faculties than do institutions with average or relatively high student-faculty ratios. In fact, we would suggest that institutions with unusually high student-faculty ratios may need to take steps designed to reduce them, difficult as this may be in underfinanced institutions.

Student-faculty ratios vary widely among groups of similar institutions (Table 12), as has already been indicated at the beginning of this section. They tend to be lower in private than in public institutions and are especially low in private liberal arts colleges, many of which would lose their specialized appeal if they were to raise their student-faculty ratios sharply. The ratios for universities are weighted, with FTE graduate enrollment given a weight of three to one for FTE undergraduate enrollment, while FTE graduate enrollment is given a weight of two for comprehensive universities and colleges. Unweighted ratios for these institutions are presented in Appendix A, Table A-6.

TABLE 12
Distribution of institutions of higher education by student-faculty ratios,* by type and control of institution, 1967–68

Ratios	Research universities		Other doctoral-granting universities		Comprehensive universities and colleges I	
	Public	Private	Public	Private	Public	Private
0–5.9						
6.0–7.9						
8.0–9.9			2.9%			
10.0–11.9		12.5%	2.9		1.2%	3.8%
12.0–13.9		24.9			2.9	6.3
14.0–15.9	4.5%	12.5	8.6	11.1%	8.8	11.4
16.0–17.9	11.4	15.6	8.6	22.2	20.0	22.7
18.0–19.9	11.4	9.4	11.4	5.6	20.7	20.3
20.0–21.9	22.7	6.3	19.8	11.1	13.5	11.4
22.0–23.9	13.6	6.3	8.6	11.1	17.6	3.8
24.0–25.9	11.4	3.1	14.3	5.6	8.8	11.4
26.0–27.9	11.4		14.3	11.1	1.8	5.1
28.0–29.9	9.1	3.1	8.6	11.1	3.5	
30.0 or more	4.5	6.3		11.1	1.2	3.8
TOTAL	100.0%	100.0%	100.0%	100.0%	100.0%	100.0%
Median	22.0%	16.0%	21.6%	22.0%	19.7%	18.6%
Number of institutions reporting	44	32†	35	18	170	79

* Senior faculty as defined in * footnote, Table 8; the weights are defined above in the text. In all other relevant tables a standard weight of three is used for graduate enrollment.

† We have excluded two institutions with small student bodies and exceptionally low student-faculty ratios.

SOURCE: Adapted from U.S. Office of Education data by Carnegie Commission staff.

There is evidence, as we noted earlier, of a relationship between student-faculty ratios and quality, at least in graduate education — student-faculty ratios are negatively related to quality, whereas if the ratios are expressed in terms of faculty to students they are positively related to quality.

But there is also very clear evidence that student-faculty ratios are positively related to institutional size as measured by FTE student enrollment (Tables C-6, C-12, C-18, and C-19, Appendix C). The relationship is less consistent, even when the ratios are computed on a weighted basis, among private universities than

Comprehensive universities and colleges II		Private liberal arts colleges I	Private liberal arts colleges II	Two-year colleges	
Public	Private			Public	Private
		0.9%	1.9%		8.7%
1.2%		3.6	2.4	0.5%	2.9
1.2	1.9%	11.7	5.8	0.9	8.1
	5.8	30.7	16.2	2.0	11.0
13.1	15.4	35.1	19.9	9.5	11.0
16.7	21.2	12.6	24.2	10.4	12.1
18.1	23.1	1.8	14.9	14.5	8.1
16.7	15.4	0.9	7.1	19.7	9.2
15.5	1.9	1.8	4.3	13.8	12.7
7.1	7.7	0.9	1.7	10.4	3.5
6.0	3.8		0.6	6.1	2.3
3.6			0.4	6.1	2.3
			0.4	1.6	2.3
1.2	3.8		0.2	4.5	5.8
100.0%	100.0%	100.0%	100.0%	100.0%	100.0%
17.9%	16.5%	12.2%	14.3%	19.2%	15.4%
84	52	111	462	441	173

among other types of institutions, but for most groups of institutions, student-faculty ratios vary more consistently with institutional size than most of the other measures included in the tables in Appendix C. The reasons are fairly obvious. A small college must have a certain minimum-sized faculty to provide its students with an adequate choice of courses and of fields of study. As it grows in size, it need not increase the size of its faculty commensurately with the increase in its student body, at least up to a point. And, especially in introductory courses, the size of classes tends to vary with the size of the institution. In very large universities, a single faculty member will often be in charge of an introductory course, lecturing to a class of as many as a thousand students several times a week and supervising the work of teaching assistants who meet with the students in small sections once or twice a week.

Thus the data in Appendix C suggest that most of the institutions with relatively low student-faculty ratios are comparatively small and some (especially among public comprehensive and two-year colleges) are probably relatively new. The problem of raising student-faculty ratios is thus closely related to the problem of achieving optimal size, which we discussed at some length in Section 3. But low student-faculty ratios can also be explained by such factors as unusually low teaching loads and exceptionally small classes, which need to be analyzed by all institutions.

On the basis of a study of the data in Table 12 and of student-faculty ratios shown in Appendix C for institutions of approximately our suggested minimum sizes in terms of FTE enrollment (Section 3),[7] we would suggest that colleges and universities need to give particular attention to measures aimed at achieving more

---

[7] We also note the following student-faculty ratios in universities in certain other nations which relate *total* students (unweighted by level) to *senior and middle* level faculty:

United Kingdom	11.7
Switzerland	13.7
Japan	14.6
Germany	20.5
Canada	24.0
Norway	33.8
Italy	54.0
France	75.4

In all these countries (except the United Kingdom) their ratios have been rising (Organization for Economic Co-operation and Development, *Study on Teachers: Quantitative Trends in Teaching Staff in Higher Education,* Paris, 1971).

effective use of faculty if their student-faculty ratios on an FTE basis are below the levels which we suggest below.

There are, of course, some small, highly selective, and relatively well financed universities and colleges that will not wish or need to raise their relatively low ratios to these levels. But there are a number, even among highly selective institutions, that are taking decisive steps to increase their student-faculty ratios — sometimes in conjunction with a shift to coeducational status as in the cases of Princeton and Williams, mentioned in Section 3.

The Commission recommends that all colleges and universities examine their utilization of faculty time and in particular that they do so if their student-faculty ratios fall below the following median levels for their categories.

Median levels below which special consideration of measures to increase student-faculty ratios may be warranted:

	Public	*Private*
Research universities	22.0 (weighted)	16.0 (weighted)
Other doctoral-granting universities	21.6 (weighted)	22.0 (weighted)
Comprehensive universities and colleges I	19.7 (weighted)	18.6 (weighted)
Comprehensive universities and colleges II	17.9 (weighted)	16.5 (weighted)
Liberal arts colleges I	*	12.2 (unweighted)
Liberal arts colleges II	*	14.3 (unweighted)
Two-year colleges	19.2 (unweighted)	15.4 (unweighted)

* There are no public liberal arts colleges I, and data have not been included on public liberal arts colleges II, because the number of these colleges reporting the necessary information was very small.

NOTE: The weight for graduate as against undergraduate students is 3 to 1 in universities and 2 to 1 in comprehensive colleges.

We believe that a careful examination of student-faculty ratios, department by department and campus by campus, can result in an overall average increase in the ratio from an unweighted 16 to an unweighted 17 without impairing educational quality.

The goal of effective use of faculty time is more likely to be accomplished through sustained attention to the many facets of the problem than through any single, sweeping change.

We recommend consideration of the following:

- Carefully studying and adopting a varied mixture of class sizes at the different levels of instruction and establishing appropriate average class sizes that different departments may be expected to meet

- Seeking to prevent undue proliferation of courses by periodic review of the totality of course offerings in a department

- Involving the faculty in developing policies directed toward achieving appropriate and equitable teaching loads

  Establishing standards relating to a reasonable maximum amount of time to be spent in consulting activities

- Maintaining reasonable and equitable policies relating to sabbatical leaves for all career members of the faculty, including assistant professors

- Analyzing costs of support personnel, in comparison with those of other similar institutions, with a view to identifying possible excessive costs in some aspects of support functions, but also of making certain that these functions are being conducted efficiently and that highly paid faculty members are not performing functions that could be delegated to lower-paid support personnel

7. Faculty Salaries and the Possible Impacts of Unionization

The deterioration in the job market for faculty members is likely to mean that faculty salaries will not rise as rapidly, relative to other wages and salaries, in the 1970s and 1980s as they did in the 1960s. From 1960 to 1970, average salaries of faculty members rose at an annual rate of 5.8 percent as compared with a rate of increase of 4.9 percent in average annual earnings per full-time employee (60, p. 85, and 61). Moreover, the annual rate of increase varied directly with rank, ranging from 5.1 percent for instructors and lecturers to 6.3 percent for full professors.

Faculty salaries are more likely in the decade ahead to rise with professional salaries generally, and these may rise at a somewhat slower rate than all wages and salaries. Professional personnel, generally, are coming into greater supply with the increased output of colleges and universities, and thus salary increases may slow down somewhat. Also, manual worker wages are rising at a particularly rapid rate. Looking at these changed circumstances, we estimate that faculty salaries (and those of other professionals) are more likely to rise at the rate of the cost of living plus 1 or 2 percent a year rather than at the rate of the cost of living plus 3 percent and more as in the 1960s, while wages and salaries generally rise at the rate of the cost of living plus 2½ or 3 percent. Since faculty salaries are about one-third of educational costs (less organized research), this will mean that costs will rise one-quarter to one-half of 1 percent less per year than in the 1960s.

However, if the slackening in the academic job market does actually result in an appreciable slowing down in the rate of increase in faculty salaries — and especially if financial stringency continues and faculty members find their employment conditions deteriorating in other ways as well — the spread of unionization among faculty members, which has been a slow development in the last few years, is likely to accelerate.

Although unionization of faculty members has spread, it is still concentrated in relatively few states where legislation favorable to collective bargaining rights of public employees in general or employees of public institutions of higher education in particular has paved the way. In the fall of 1971, Garbarino estimated that there were 133 public institutions of higher education with recognized bargaining units in 15 states (including the District of Columbia and Guam), but 118 of these were concentrated in 6 states — Illinois, Massachusetts, Michigan, New Jersey, New York, and Wisconsin. Covered by these units were some 45,000 to 50,000 persons. But Garbarino also commented:

These data understate the importance of collective negotiations for faculty for at least three reasons: (1) the data are inevitably incomplete; (2) the entries are representation *units,* not *campuses,* e.g., SUNY with 26 component campuses appears as one unit; and (3) only situations in which formal, usually exclusive, recognition of a single bargaining agent has been granted are counted. In hundreds of other institutions, local units of faculty organizations exist and have a variety of less formal arrangements for recognition and consultation. Of some 1,800 institutions responding to a National Education Association survey in 1969–70, 766 reported that they maintained "a formal procedure . . . by which representatives of the governing board" agreed to confer with faculty representatives on matters of salary or welfare (62).

The Carnegie Commission Survey of Students and Faculty, 1969, revealed that 60 percent of faculty members disagreed with the statement that "collective bargaining has no place in a college or university." Younger faculty members were considerably less opposed to collective bargaining than older faculty members, with 72 percent of those aged 30 or less disagreeing with the statement, as compared with 51 percent of those older than 50.[1] Active support for unionism among younger faculty members is particularly likely to grow in the 1970s under academic job market conditions that will have a more adverse effect on young academicians than on older, tenured faculty members.

[1] Included in these percentages are those who responded that they "strongly disagreed" or "disagreed with reservations" with the statement.

Thus, administrators in many institutions of higher education—especially in large public systems of higher education—will need to prepare themsleves to establish successful collective bargaining relationships. This means, among other things, employing staff members or consultants who are experienced in collective bargaining on the management side. The results will not necessarily be altogether adverse to efforts to achieve effective use of resources. The union contract can be a means by which some costs are made more certain, as compared with free-flowing actions of faculty members; it becomes an instrument for more centralized control. It may also be possible for "management" to achieve provisions designed to increase faculty productivity, e.g., modest increases in teaching loads in return for increases in salaries and fringe benefits—as happens in other segments of society. But it may become more difficult to maintain high standards for faculty appointments and promotions. As Garbarino points out, it seems probable "that in those key institutions in which the untidy, unsystematic process of peer evaluation has worked with demonstrated success, the introduction of procedures that can be defended before an arbitrator, or perhaps a judge, will incur a real cost in quality" (62).

One of the complications of collective bargaining in state universities and colleges, of course, is that the costs of concessions to union members will ultimately have to be met by increased state appropriations in most situations. Thus, the institutions' management representatives in bargaining situations are likely to find themselves dealing also with representatives of the governor's office. This is all the more reason for employing specialized negotiators who develop ongoing relationships with both any union or unions and representatives of the governor's office.

The Commission recommends that institutions of higher education engaged with faculty unionism employ staff members or consultants who are experienced in collective bargaining negotiations and consider the possibility of agreements that will induce increases in the productivity of faculty members and other academic employees without impairing educational effectiveness.

8. Achieving Budgetary Flexibility

A critical problem facing colleges and universities in this period of budgetary stringency is how to achieve budgetary flexibility. An institution of higher education cannot serve its students effectively with a static program mix. Its program must be dynamic and responsive, not only to changes in the job market for college graduates but also to advances in knowledge and to changing student interests and concerns.

When both enrollment and income were growing rapidly, as was the case throughout the greater part of the 1960s, adaptation to changing needs could be achieved with relative ease. Incremental funds could be allocated mainly to the schools and departments in which rapid growth in enrollment was occurring. The very process of growth makes for budgetary flexibility. Salary savings accrue, because it takes time to fill newly authorized positions and to replace faculty members who retire or resign. These salary savings can be channeled to other parts of the budget in which augmented funds are needed (although state institutions in some cases are required to allow all or part of salary savings to revert to the state treasury). An increased flow of research funds also makes it possible to meet a portion of faculty salaries from research budgets and provides increased opportunities for the employment of graduate research assistants.

When budgetary stringency develops, flexibility is much more difficult to achieve. Salary savings tend to decline when it becomes necessary to curtail the hiring of new faculty. Universities that have met faculty salaries from "soft" (extramural research) money—and this practice was considerably more prevalent in private than in public research universities in the 1960s—may suddenly find their faculty salary budgets inadequate to cover the salaries of tenured professors when the flow of research funds levels off or declines.

More basically, funds must be found to develop new programs or expand existing programs in response to changing needs. In a period of budgetary stringency, this may well necessitate curtailing or dropping programs for which demand has declined or in which the institution has not developed great strength.[1]

The need for flexibility will be particularly critical in the 1970s because of the dramatic changes that are occurring in the job market for college graduates. Not only is the overall job market for highly educated manpower expected to be less favorable throughout the 1970s than it has been during the greater part of the postwar period, but also pronounced shifts are occurring in the relative markets for jobseekers trained in various fields. Because the children now entering elementary school were born in years in which the absolute number of births was declining, a surplus of elementary and secondary school teachers is developing and is likely to become an increasingly serious problem in the coming years. The supply of Ph.D.'s has caught up with, and in many fields has overtaken, the demand, and the problem of a surplus of Ph.D.'s, in relation to demand in the types of positions formerly acceptable to Ph.D.'s, is predicted to become more serious in the course of the 1970s. This will have undesirable repercussions on the demand for holders of less-advanced degrees, as Ph.D.'s accept positions that would formerly have been filled by holders of bachelor's and master's degrees. Conflicting predictions are being made as to whether the current surplus of scientists and engineers will disappear or become a more serious problem in the course of the 1970s. Meanwhile, there are shortages of professional personnel in the health sciences, and favorable job markets are expected to continue in such fields as urban planning, social work, counseling, and various occupations in local government.

However, changing programmatic needs are by no means exclusively related to shifts in the job market. The growing interest in ecology, for example, is not as yet attributable to any very pronounced increase in the number of jobs available in that field, and yet few educators would argue that students should be denied the opportunity to study environmental problems or that the current trend toward adoption of federal and state legislation aimed at protection of the environment will not eventually lead to a substan-

---

[1] It is important to recognize, as indicated at a later point, that phasing out programs takes time because of commitments to students and staff.

tial increase in demand for professional workers trained in environmental fields.

In fact, students are displaying great sensitivity to changes in the labor market in their choice of fields, but they are also enrolling in greatly increased numbers in courses of study relating to environmental problems and to the urban crisis. The Carnegie Commission Fall 1971 Enrollment Survey revealed sharp declines between 1970 and 1971 in first-time undergraduate enrollment in engineering and education, along with sharp increases in first-time enrollment in forestry, social work, nursing, and biological sciences (63). At the graduate level, there was also a drop in engineering enrollment, along with especially pronounced increases in enrollment in architecture, nursing, urban studies, psychology, and biological sciences. Also noteworthy was a modest increase in graduate enrollment in education in the face of a deteriorating job market for teachers, suggesting that college graduates who were failing to find teaching jobs were returning for graduate work in education in the hope of improving their job prospects.[2]

The difficulty in achieving budgetary flexibility is likely to become even more critical in the 1980s, when total enrollment in higher education is expected to become essentially stationary, unless the impact of the decline in the college-age population is more than offset by increased enrollment of adults. If overall enrollment is stationary, institutions will face problems in attempting to convince federal, state, and private agencies that increased funds will continue to be needed even to cover rising costs of education per student, let alone adopt new programs. The budgets of institutions of higher education are likely to be very tight, and yet adaptation to changing programmatic needs will continue to be of critical importance.

In fact, the prospect of essentially stationary enrollment in the 1980s requires that colleges and universities that have been experiencing rapid growth begin planning now for the adjustments that will have to be made in a period of slow or nonexistent growth. But it will also be important for state planning agencies, as well as individual institutions, to take account of the fact that enrollment

---

[2] Also a familiar phenomenon in the last few years has been a sharp increase in applications to law and medical schools, but this has been accompanied by only relatively modest increases in enrollment because of the limited capacity of the schools. However, medical schools in particular have been increasing the size of their entering classes at an impressive rate in the last few years.

in some institutions, especially comprehensive colleges and community colleges located in areas experiencing net in-migration, may continue to grow, while similar institutions in areas characterized by net out-migration are likely to experience declining enrollment. Continuous analysis of population changes will be more important than ever.

There are at least six general approaches that are being used by institutions of higher education to achieve cutbacks in some programs in order to release funds for expansion in others or for the development of new programs. These are (1) selective cutbacks, (2) across-the-board percentage cuts in budgets, (3) consolidation of existing programs, (4) readaptation of existing programs, (5) application of Harvard University's "every tub on its own bottom" approach, and (6) central reassignment of vacated positions. In practice, various combinations of these approaches are being used. These varying strategies are, of course, available on a multicampus basis, as well as in single-campus institutions, but in multicampus institutions, a major objective will be to achieve flexibility in the distribution of funds among campuses, as well as among schools and departments within campuses.

SELECTIVE CUTBACKS   Selective cutbacks based on careful analysis of needs for existing programs have been emphasized at Princeton, Stanford, and other institutions—usually along with more general approaches, such as a freeze on the total number of faculty. Cutbacks are seldom painless and present special difficulties when curtailment affects tenured faculty and term contracts. Because of contractual obligations, cutbacks can be accomplished only gradually in some cases.

The most important general question in relation to selective cutbacks concerns the criteria to be used. One of the most obvious is declining enrollment in a field. Where there has been a long-run tendency toward a decline in enrollment, curtailment may be indicated, but there are also possibilities of inducing faculty members to broaden their interests and to teach a somewhat different group of courses.

Caution is needed when a decline in enrollment is not clearly associated with a long-run downward trend. Engineering is a case in point. Throughout the postwar period, there have been pronounced fluctuations in the job market for engineers, which have induced corresponding fluctuations in enrollment in engineering in institutions of higher education. As Freeman (64) and others have shown, there is clearly a "cobweb" effect, in the economist's terms, at work. When the demand for engineers increases sharply, students flock into undergraduate engineering majors, and before very long the increased supply of engineers begins to overtake the increase in demand, starting salaries for engineers level off, jobs in engineering become more difficult to find, and the flow of students into engineering schools declines. But the long-run trend in an increasingly complex industrial society is toward a rise in the ratio of engineers to population. Hence a surplus in the job market for engineers is likely to be followed sooner or later by an emerging scarcity. Because there are at present a number of conflicting predictions with respect to the future job market for engineers (65, 66, and 67), we would urge colleges and universities not to overreact to the current surplus by curtailing engineering programs sharply. Rather, they should aim at long-run stability in the capacity of engineering programs. Similar considerations relate to natural science fields in which there are current surpluses of graduates.

A more general problem, exemplifying a danger of overreaction to factors tending to depress enrollment, is the recent trend toward deliberate curtailment of graduate enrollment at some of the leading research universities, including Harvard, Princeton, Yale, the University of California at Berkeley, and the University of Wisconsin at Madison (68). In part, this has represented a response to the reduced flow of research funds and to a sharp curtailment in the number of graduate fellowships available, not only because of cutbacks in federal government fellowship programs, but also because of such developments as discontinuation of the Woodrow Wilson Foundation graduate fellowship program and the curtailment of the Ford Foundation fellowship programs. The deterioration in the job market for Ph.D.'s has also been an important factor influencing decisions to cut back on fellowship programs. On the other hand, the University of Chicago has been struggling, not entirely successfully, to maintain its graduate enrollment in the face of these trends (69).

While a number of leading research universities are curtailing graduate programs, many nondoctoral institutions are seeking to develop doctoral programs (70), and the Commission's recent survey of enrollment patterns indicated that, between the fall of 1970 and the fall of 1971, both public and private colleges experienced a substantially greater percentage increase in postbaccalaureate enrollment than either public or private universities—with the private universities reporting a slight decrease in first-time graduate enrollment (63).

We believe that these trends are unfortunate and that, if they continue, they will be detrimental, not only to the quality of graduate education but also to effective use of resources in graduate education. There are significant economies of scale in graduate programs, and the proliferation of doctoral-granting institutions is likely to result in increased overall average costs per student as well as in deterioration of quality.

Although general cutbacks in graduate programs at leading research universities are undesirable, carefully considered selective cutbacks may be desirable in some cases. In seeking selective cutbacks, the Priorities Committee at Princeton University developed a very carefully considered set of criteria for evaluating graduate programs:

1 The quality of the faculty and of the program of graduate instruction, as they can be inferred from the opinion of other scholars in the field, the views of faculty members in related disciplines at Princeton, and any available evidence based on the opinions and experiences of graduate students

2 The number and quality of students who have applied for graduate study at Princeton in the field, who have accepted admission, and who have completed the program

3 The future of the whole field of study in terms of scientific and scholarly trends and in terms of national needs

4 The national contribution of the Princeton graduate program, viewed in the context of the number of other strong programs, whether or not they are operating below their desirable size, and, in general, whether suspension of a program at Princeton would have a seriously adverse effect on opportunities for graduate study

5 The comparative advantage of Princeton in the field—that is, the ability of Princeton to make a particular contribution to the field in question because of special factors such as a long tradition of good work in the subject, unusually strong library resources, and so on

6 The interactions between graduate study in the field in question and graduate work and scholarship in other fields at Princeton, and the likely effects of suspending work in the field on other programs and faculty members

7 The interaction between graduate study in the field and the quality and variety of undergraduate offerings in the same field

8   The costliness of work in the field, measured in terms of instructional costs, student support, library costs, space costs, and so on (58, p. 52)

Applying these criteria, the Priorities Committee recommended the discontinuation of the Ph.D. program (but not undergraduate or master's programs) in slavic languages in the spring of 1971. A major factor influencing this decision was the very high library cost per student associated with this Ph.D. program. However, early in 1972 the Committee, modifying an earlier recommendation, called for stabilization of *total* graduate enrollment at about 1,300 students—a goal which would require a sizable increase in graduate student support from endowment and general funds to replace diminishing extramural sources of support for graduate students (71, pp. 26–33).

More drastic selective cutbacks in graduate programs have occurred at Tulane University, where Ph.D. programs were eliminated in the fields of classics, Italian, geology, music, theater, and social work, while St. Louis University closed its School of Dentistry and its four engineering departments (5, pp. 99–100).

The Commission recommends that leading research universities refrain from cutbacks in graduate programs except on a carefully considered, selective basis. We also recommend that institutions with less emphasis on research consider curtailment or elimination, on a selective basis, of Ph.D. programs that are not of high quality or that are too small to be operated economically. We urge great caution in the development of new Ph.D. programs in particular fields at existing doctoral-granting institutions and do not believe that there is a need for any new Ph.D.-granting institutions, although some or even many institutions will be introducing the D.A. degree.

Illustrative of selective cutback programs that have achieved significant economies are those at the Massachusetts Institute of Technology, New York University, Stanford University, and the University of California. Details on just how these economies were (or were to be) achieved are available in the documents cited in connection with the following summaries:

Massachusetts Institute of Technology   MIT was forced to take decisive action in the fall of 1971, when it faced a budgetary deficit of $6 million for the fiscal year 1971–72. Selective budgetary cuts amounting to $4 million out of a total budget of approximately $70 million were planned (72).

New York University Among the more difficult fiscal problems of any private university in the country are those of NYU, which has been experiencing growing budgetary deficits since the mid-1960s. Budgetary cuts achieved on the basis of the work of its Commission on Effective Use of Resources saved $3.5 million of expenditures in the 1970–71 budget. This saving, combined with a change in the method of computing income from endowment funds (aimed at gradually benefiting from capital gains), was expected to reduce the 1970–71 deficit from the initially projected $9.5 million to $4.5 million (73). However, in the fall of 1971 President James Hester announced that the final deficit for 1970–71 was $6.7 million and that the deficit for 1971–72 might be as large as $10 million (74).

Princeton University For the fiscal year 1971–72, budgetary cuts recommended by the Priorities Committee after extensive study resulted in savings of $2.6 million out of an initially proposed budget of $76.9 million. Changes designed to bring about an increase in income of $1.7 million, chiefly through increases in student fees, also contributed to a reduction in the anticipated deficit for the fiscal year from $5.5 million to $1.2 million (58, p. 25).

For fiscal 1972–73, the Priorities Committee developed a group of additional recommendations which were expected to reduce the deficit for that year to about $0.5 million. Their plans for subsequent fiscal years contemplated a balanced budget for 1973–74 and very small deficits in the following two years (71, p. 19).

Stanford University Stanford's Budget Adjustment Program, initiated in October 1969, is designed to eliminate a cumulative deficit of $6 million over a five-year period. Phase I was concerned with efforts to reduce an anticipated deficit of approximately $1.5 million in fiscal year 1970–71. The targeted budget reduction was $950,000 out of a total budget of $57 million, and the reduction actually achieved was $978,000 (75). For fiscal 1971–72, the economies planned under the Budget Adjustment Program were designed to achieve expenditure reductions of $1,264,000 (76).

University of California The University of California has been facing a series of increasingly stringent budgets since 1967–68. It has responded by increasing the student-faculty ratio, eliminating faculty positions, and imposing drastic economies on such functions as library and maintenance operations. The magnitude of the adjustments that have been required is clearly indicated by data on changes in enrollment-related costs per FTE student financed from state funds (77, p. 61):

Enrollment-related costs per FTE student, state funds, general campuses, University of California	Current dollars	Percent change from 1966-67	Constant 1970-71 dollars	Percent change from 1966-67
1966–67 actual	$1,839		$2,209	
1967–68 actual	1,809	−1.6%	2,055	− 7.0%
1968–69 actual	1,826	−0.7	1,969	−10.9
1969–70 budget	1,842	0.2	1,886	−14.6
1970–71 budget	1,830	−0.5	1,830	−17.2

According to Dr. George Weathersby of the Office of the Vice President for Planning and Analysis, the reduction in costs per FTE student in constant dollars amounted to 20 percent by the fall of 1971.

ACROSS-THE-BOARD CUTS Across-the-board budgetary cuts may be essential in an emergency, but are not particularly desirable as a sustained response to budgetary stringency unless they are deliberately designed, at least in part, to release funds which the central administration can channel into new and expanding programs. If used for the latter purpose, they have some advantages over selective cutbacks, although we would certainly not regard the two approaches as mutually exclusive, and in practice they are not. Across-the-board cuts require less initial study than selective cutbacks and are likely to be accepted as more equitable. Each school and department is impelled to examine its operation carefully and may be able to identify relatively painless economies that would be difficult for a campuswide advisory committee or central administration to uncover.

Perhaps the most decisive application of this approach that has come to our attention is at Case-Western Reserve University, which was experiencing particularly severe budgetary deficits until it began to "turn the situation around" in 1970. President Louis A. Toepfer has provided us with the following description of how this program has operated during its first two years:

This University established a plan to eliminate approximately $2,000,000 of expense over income in each of two successive years, while absorbing salary increases and other cost increases. This was achieved by a combination of expense reduction and income increases. In the first year across-the-board income and expense targets were assigned to each area of the institution proportional to the level of activity. Area managers were encouraged not only to absorb the impact of rising costs, and increase incomes, but also encouraged to reduce expenses below target levels, thereby gaining internal area funding redistribution flexibility. The impact of this program was to free up approximately 10 percent of operating expense. Approximately 5 percent of free funds were used to reduce the deficit, the other 5 percent was used to absorb normal cost increases for salaries, heat and light, that would have occurred in any case.

In the second year of the program, the targets for further expense reduction, expense absorption and additional income were assigned. The targets at this stage were more selective, recognizing area differences and less specific in order to allow increased area management flexibility.

The principal advantage of this program and its intent has been to eliminate as quickly as possible unfundable deficits which absorb all new income and paralyze realistic program planning and realignment. From a position of fiscal balance selective program reductions and expansions can be made and the use of savings and new incomes towards program development and expansion becomes feasible.

This is a very difficult program to carry out successfully. As institutions that have been facing budgetary stringency for some years have learned, with each successive year, economies become more difficult to achieve — the earliest economies, in other words, are easier to identify and enforce than those that come later. As a consequence, the effectiveness of this type of program is greatest in the early years, and should be used to accomplish a planned change in budgetary activity to a new level over a relatively short time period.

A similar approach is being used at the University of Minnesota, which was faced with a reduction of 5 percent in legislative appropriations (not including salary increases) between 1970–71 and 1971–72, and with another 0.5 percent reduction for 1972–73. The university administration responded with an across-the-board budgetary cut for 1971–72. For 1972–73, however, an across-the-board budgetary reduction of 6 percent was imposed in order both to carry out the mandatory retrenchment and to achieve some reallocation of funds to schools and departments with special needs for augmentation. Of the total 6 percent cut, 0.5 percent was to be allocated to Educational Development Funds, destined for new programs (78). Similarly, across-the-board reductions designed at least partly to achieve reallocation of funds have been adopted at the University of Iowa, the University of Michigan, and the University of Washington (79, p. 7, and 80).

The concept of an educational development fund has also been adopted at Stanford University, where a University Progress Fund of $200,000 for new programs of instruction was established in 1971–72, and where there also was instituted a Research Development Fund of $200,000 in 1971–72 to support new directions in research. The latter fund was to be regarded as providing "seed" money to be used while long-term outside funding is solicited (76).

CONSOLI-DATING EXISTING PROGRAMS Within universities, and perhaps occasionally in other types of institutions, there are situations in which quite substantial economies can be achieved by consolidation of overlapping and duplicating programs. For example, there are, often, costly duplications of faculty specialties and equipment between basic science departments in medical centers and on main campuses. Although consolidation of such departments has been very difficult to accomplish in the past, the growing interest in integration of premedical and medical education, and of predental and dental education, as part of the trend toward acceleration of medical and dental education may mean that there will be more progress in the future in accomplishing integration in these fields.

A particularly complex problem of overlapping and duplication of programs confronted Case-Western Reserve University after the merger of Case Institute and Western Reserve University. In some of the basic sciences there were three departments—one formerly in Case Institute, a second in Western Reserve University, and a third in the medical school of Western Reserve. This has made for very high faculty-student ratios in these fields in the merged university—a problem that can be overcome only gradually through a process of attrition because of obligations to tenured faculty members.

Another glaring example of overlapping and duplication was described recently by President William J. McGill of Columbia University as follows:

There is a psychology department in the graduate faculties. There is an entirely different one at Teachers College, an entirely different one at Barnard. There is a quite different psychology department at the College of Physicians and Surgeons. This is an intolerable situation (81).

READAPTING CERTAIN PROGRAMS Programs in which interest is declining can sometimes be readapted to meet new needs. One of the most promising examples is the possibility of broadening the programs of colleges of agriculture and forestry to place greater emphasis on environmental problems. This is happening on the Berkeley Campus of the University of California, where the Department of Forestry and Conservation offers a number of courses concerned with environmental problems, some of them jointly with the Department of Agricultural Economics and with the Interdepartmental Studies Program.

The problem of declining enrollment in many other fields, however, will present greater difficulties.

EVERY TUB ON ITS OWN BOTTOM At Harvard University, a considerable degree of budgetary flexibility is achieved through a longstanding policy — dubbed ETOB or "every tub on its own bottom" — under which every school or college is expected to develop its own resources. Thus, if the medical school has a plan for expansion, which is approved by the governing board, it must seek the funds to support the expansion. In this case such funds would probably be forthcoming from a combination of federal government and private sources. This does not mean that the central administration has no power to influence the process of decision making over the relative expansion or contraction of schools or departments. The president can often influence donors to give money for a purpose deemed important by the central administration, and some "old money" is unrestricted (82, p. 8).

This policy, in general, can be expected to achieve budgetary flexibility of a desirable sort, because those schools and departments representing fields in which there are manpower shortages and challenging emerging social problems undoubtedly stand a better chance of raising funds than those in which enrollment and interest are declining. However, the policy is probably better adapted to leading private research universities than to other groups of institutions. Stanford has moved toward a similar policy in relation to its School of Medicine and its Graduate School of Business. Under this "allocation by formula" policy, the School of Medicine, for example, relies significantly on its own resources and receives allocations within the university's operating budget on the basis of enrollment and tuition (76). Columbia has also made use of this general approach. As a general budgetary strategy, however, it has its limitations and may in some cases encourage excessive decentralization. The "tub" approach is most useful in encouraging each school or college to raise the maximum amount of money it can and to use it effectively. But it can impede redistribution of funds within the institution as a whole.

**REALLOCA-
TION OF
VACATED
POSITIONS** A sixth way of getting flexibility is to require that all positions vacated through resignation, retirement, or death be allocated back to the central administration, rather than being kept by the individual department or school, so that the central administration may determine where the need for reassignment is greatest. It is important that positions vacated on the initiative of the department not revert, however, else the department may be inclined to keep people it really does not want and should not have.

The Commission recommends that all institutions of higher education place emphasis on policies that will ensure budgetary flexibility. Combinations of policies that will achieve this goal will vary from institution to institution but may well include elements of (1) selective cutbacks, (2) across-the-board budgetary cuts, (3) consolidation of existing programs, (4) readaptation of existing programs, (5) "every tub on its own bottom," and (6) central reassignment of positions vacated due to resignation, retirement, or death.

During the greater part of the 1960s, when both enrollment and expenditures were rising rapidly in higher education, new programs were frequently adopted without careful evaluation of their long-run costs. Under various kinds of pressures, programs were started in ethnic studies, environmental problems, water resources, urban affairs, and other fields. This is not to suggest that there was not a good case for development of these programs in most instances, but the initial costs were in some cases met through allocations of special funds by boards of trustees, presidents, or chief campus administrators without careful study of the ultimate costs of the program or of the probability of development of "harder" sources of funds over the long pull. There is little question that in many institutions the financial crisis has been more difficult to bring under control than would otherwise have been the case because of expansion into these new fields. In the future, colleges and universities will be forced to exercise more caution in adopting new programs and would be well advised not only to develop data on long-run costs and sources of funding but also to staff new and experimental programs to a considerable extent with temporary personnel until some experience has been gained and firm sources of financing obtained.

Whether or not an institution is experiencing financial stringency, there is a strong case for periodic, or even more or less continuous, programmatic review, especially in relatively large colleges, universities, and multicampus institutions. In fact, some state coordinating councils are insisting on such review, with a view particularly to eliminating degree programs that cannot be operated economically because relatively few degrees are awarded.

Where state coordinating councils or boards have regulatory rather than advisory powers, these powers frequently include the power to prevent the establishment of new programs or to require discontinuation of existing programs.

Clearly, within a large state college or state university system, there is a great deal to be said for policies that are designed to confine degree programs that tend to be relatively costly and/or to attract relatively few students to only one or two campuses within the system.

Colleges and universities that are not a part of large public systems are often in a position to achieve a similar objective through consortium arrangements with neighboring institutions or by contracting with another appropriate institution to offer a given program to their students. There is room for much more progress in this direction than has been achieved to date.

The Commission recommends that colleges and universities use great caution in adopting new degree programs and conduct periodic reviews of existing degree programs, with a view to eliminating those in which very few degrees are awarded, whether or not they are required to do so by state coordinating bodies. Coordinating bodies may also need to conduct such review if the institutions fail in their responsibilities. In multicampus institutions, there is a strong case for confining highly specialized degree programs to only one or two campuses within the system.[3]

Where programmatic cutbacks must be achieved, particularly when they are made on a selective basis, it may be desirable for the institution to develop a decision-making process that involves faculty and students along with representatives of the administration in the decision-making process in an advisory capacity. If

---

[3] The tables in Appendix C indicate that the number of fields in which degrees are offered rises sharply with increasing enrollment in private universities and in comprehensive universities and colleges. The number of fields also rises sharply in public universities (data not shown).

faculty members and students thoroughly understand why cut-backs must be achieved and why particular programs were selected for curtailment or discontinuation, the decisions are likely to be more acceptable than when more traditional administrative procedures are followed. Also, such advice may (1) lead to a greater sense of cost-consciousness on the part of the academic community, (2) identify those functions which are most and least cherished by faculty members and students, and (3) identify possible trade-offs as, for example, between higher teaching loads and higher salaries. Committees have been successfully used at Princeton and New York University. They do, however, require the availability of a great deal of data and the expenditure of much administrative time. Hearings are alternatives.

The commission recommends that institutions of higher education consider the establishment of committees including faculty, students, and administrators to serve in an advisory capacity in relation to the preparation of the budget when severe cuts must be made. Where it is not considered feasible or desirable to establish such committees, the more traditional practice of holding hearings on major budgetary decisions can provide faculty and students with opportunities to express their views.

We consider it essential that some existing funds each year be made available for new or expanded endeavors. We believe that 1 to 3 percent a year can be so provided each year on most campuses and can be effectively used.

The Commission recommends that colleges and universities develop a "self-renewal" fund of 1 to 3 percent each year taken from existing allocations.

9. Incentives for Constructive Change and Innovation

One obstacle to the achievement of effective use of resources in higher education is the fact that compensation and budgetary procedures are not structured in such a way as to induce change. In private industry, innovations that achieve savings in production costs tend to improve the firm's competitive position and to increase profits, which, under profit-sharing schemes, will benefit the firm's executives. No such mechanism exists in higher education or in most nonprofit organizations. In fact, budgetary procedures tend to discourage innovations to save costs.

Under typical budgetary procedures, a department or school wishing to acquire more efficient duplicating equipment, for example, must first persuade the administration to permit inclusion of the item in its "equipment and facilities" budget for a given year. If the item is costly, this may be difficult. Suppose it is approved, and the equipment, once installed, has the effect of reducing the department's need for clerical workers by one full-time position. No benefit accrues to the department by simply allowing that salary item to disappear from its budget for the following year, so it is likely to seek a way of using the FTE position for some other purpose.

A preferable way of handling such an investment might be for the department to submit a proposal indicating the savings that could be achieved through installation of the new equipment, and for the administration to permit a significant proportion of the savings to be retained by the department. The capital cost of the new equipment would not appear in the departmental budget, but only in the budget of the central administration. The departmental budget would include a rental charge for the equipment against which any savings achieved would be measured. Part of the difference between the rental charge and the salary savings—for example, one-half—would be retained by the department with "no strings" attached as to how the savings would be used. Alternatively, the department might be required in its original proposal to indicate how the savings would be used.

Another factor operating against efforts of departments and schools to achieve effective use of resources, especially in public institutions, is the rigid annual departmental budget, under which any unspent balances revert to the central administration and, often, to a large extent, to the state treasury under state budgetary requirements.

Departments and schools frequently can anticipate salary savings in a given year, because faculty members are on leave, or because past experience indicates that lags in the replacement of academic or nonacademic employees who resign in the course of a year will generate salary savings. Typically departments and schools will find ways of using those salary savings to hire temporary personnel, even though in some cases the temporary personnel may not be vitally needed to maintain the department's usual course offerings or other services. Otherwise it will "lose the savings." This is also true of research institutes and centers, where ways can almost always be found for using an additional research assistant or clerical employee. Similarly, if there is a balance in the department's "supplies and expense" account as the close of the academic year approaches, the department typically will find ways of spending it.

Budgetary procedures in state institutions are designed to restrict the expenditure of salary and other savings by schools and departments, but they are not very effective because it is generally not very difficult to demonstrate a need for temporary personnel or other kinds of expenditures, or just to make expenditures for them as a fait accompli. Furthermore, restrictive regulations tend to generate costs in the form of bureaucratic "red tape." The budgetary stringency of the last few years has resulted in attempts to tighten up on restrictive regulations of this sort, and, of course, as we suggested earlier, conditions were far more favorable for the generation of salary and other kinds of savings during the rapid growth years of the 1960s than they have been in the last few years. Even so, there may well be possibilities of savings, especially in departments in which enrollment is stationary or declining, that are not realized because there is no incentive for departments or schools to attempt to realize them.

We believe that the answer to this problem, especially in large institutions, is not to impose more bureaucratic restrictions and surveillance methods designed to overcome these secretive methods of departments and schools, but rather to provide incentives for economies by allowing departments to carry over a significant proportion of unspent balances from year to year. In some cases, this might well tend to hold down departmental budgetary requests, and it would almost certainly result in more prudent and carefully planned expenditures. There would be no reason to rush into expenditures that were not required at the moment.

Ways and means should be devised to provide monetary rewards to individual employees who make constructive suggestions for changes or innovations that result in economies, as is frequently done in private industry. In recent years, there has been a very desirable trend toward providing monetary awards for faculty members who are identified as outstandingly successful teachers, but we know of no such trend toward awards for administrators or academic employees who suggest innovations that will induce economies. However, some institutions do have such awards for nonacademic employees.

As suggested in Section 3, also, departments and schools should be expected to justify budgetary requests on the basis, not only of input measures (e.g., enrollment), but also on the basis of output or performance criteria.

It may be desirable to assign some significant proportion of savings to projects of interest to faculty members, such as salary increases or library acquisitions, and of interest to students, such as a lowered increase in tuition or an increase in scholarship funds.

The Commission recommends that institutions of higher education seek to alter their budgetary procedures in such a way as to induce cost-saving change, giving special attention to the possibilities of permitting departments and schools to carry over from year to year significant proportions of unspent balances in their budgets and of permitting them to retain a portion of the budgetary savings resulting from innovation or investment in more efficient equipment. Ways and means of providing monetary compensation, probably principally in the form of special awards, for employees who make constructive suggestions for innovations that result in economies should be developed.

Because changes in budgetary procedures in public institutions of higher education will often require changes in state legislation or administrative regulations, it may be necessary for institutions to seek permission to carry out pilot projects designed to demonstrate that changes in procedures will yield economies. The Commission recommends that state coordinating councils and boards seek to encourage such projects.

We note the successful policy of the state of Tennessee in allowing the University of Tennessee to keep all of its budgetary savings.

10. Special Problems of a Period of Declining Rate of Growth

One of the most important factors in any attempt to arrive at effective use of resources is the achievement of flexibility in the use of faculty. This will be far more difficult to achieve in the period of declining rate of growth which we face in the 1970s and of almost stationary enrollment which we shall face in the 1980s than in the unprecedentedly rapid growth rate years of the 1960s. Enrollment may rise at a steadily declining rate from 1970 to 1982, decline slightly in absolute terms from 1982 to 1987, and then begin to rise again. From about 1974 on, the students entering college will have been born in a period of declining birthrates, and, from about 1978 on, the college entrants will have been born in a period when the absolute number of live births was declining. Thus, although we expect enrollment rates as a percentage of the age group to continue to rise in the 1970s and 1980s, the decline in the size of the age cohorts will eventually more than offset the impact of rising enrollment rates. Changes in the projected annual rate of increase in FTE enrollment to 1990 are presented in Chart 5.

The effect on the demand for faculty will be dramatic. As the rate of growth in enrollment declines, the need for additions to faculty will also taper off. Turnover of faculty members will undoubtedly decline as new hiring falls off, and in the 1980s additional faculty members will be needed only to replace those who retire or who die before retirement.

It is possible, of course, that the trend toward increased enrollment rates of adults in higher education could lead to more rapid growth in the 1970s than our projections suggest and to some growth in the 1980s. However, it does not seem likely that this trend could change appreciably the outlook in the job market for faculty members. For one thing, if young people "stop out" to an increasing extent with a view to returning later, some of the in-

CHART 5 *Annual percentage change in full-time equivalent enrollment in higher education, actual, 1969–70, and projected, 1970–1990*

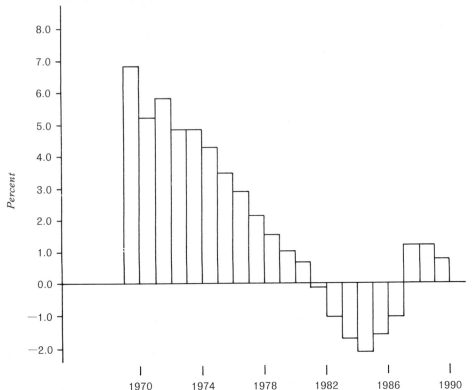

SOURCE: Projections developed for the Carnegie Commission by Gus W. Haggstrom of the University of California, Berkeley. The projections have recently been revised (from 1986 on) to reflect the behavior of the birthrate in the last few years.

crease in enrollment of adults will merely replace losses in enrollment of some college-age youth. For another, the adults are likely to be enrolled in many instances in external degree and open university programs, which will be likely to rely heavily on part-time faculty and to have high student-faculty ratios.

Assuming, then, that the demand for faculty tapers off and then declines, institutions will nevertheless not be able to "settle" for a static program mix. Students will be entering some fields of study in increasing numbers and other fields in declining numbers. Ideally, the supply of faculty should adjust to these changing needs, but this will be difficult to accomplish in a period when colleges and universities will not be able to justify overall increases in their faculties. The problem is closely related to that of achieving budgetary flexibility, already discussed, but it takes on special dimensions when we consider the impact on faculty, partly because the proportion of tenured faculty members will tend to rise in a period of declining growth, and partly because highly educated faculty members cannot shift their fields of specialization with ease.

Nevertheless, shifts to neighboring or related fields can be accomplished, and universities and colleges may have to devise ways to encourage their faculty members, on a voluntary basis, to engage in retraining to facilitate such shifts. If, for example, colleges of agriculture become more concerned with the environment, faculty members will have to engage in a certain amount of reeducation in prolems relating to the environment, but fortunately in this case their basic training in the fields typically represented in colleges of agriculture is likely to be reasonably appropriate.

Shifts out of some fields of declining enrollment may be more difficult to accomplish. In some of these cases it may be possible to find nonteaching assignments for some of the faculty members involved—e.g., in the administration. Colleges and universities may also have to take more initiative in attempts to solicit job offers for their faculty members from other institutions.

During the first half of the 1970s when enrollment will continue to increase at an appreciable rate, colleges and universities may want to consider meeting needs for increased faculty, at least to some degree, by appointing part-time faculty members and other types of temporary faculty personnel. Thus they will be able to meet the stationary enrollment period of the 1980s with relatively fewer tenured faculty than if they create many new career positions in the coming years. According to Assistant Chancellor Errol Mauchlan, the Berkeley Campus of the University of California has been able to weather the current period of financial stringency with less pain than might otherwise have been felt, because in the rapid growth years of the early 1960s, as enrollment rose toward the impending ceiling, relatively extensive use was made of visiting faculty members and lecturers. This was not so much a matter of deliberate campus policy as it was a result of the enforcement of high standards in career appointments, with the result that there was often a considerable delay in making such appointments.[1]

On the other hand, it will be important for colleges and universi-

---

[1] The campus, however, has recently been criticized for discriminating against women by retaining many of them as lecturers and refusing to appoint them to career positions (83).

ties to provide permanent employment opportunities for able young scholars and to make certain that there is a continual flow of recently trained young talent into their faculties. As enrollment stabilizes, such appointments will have to be largely limited to replacement of faculty members who die or retire. But faculty members have relatively low mortality rates, and, overall, only about 1.5 percent of all senior faculty members have to be replaced annually. It is for this reason that we suggest the importance of considering policies that will encourage voluntary early retirement later in this section.

For a variety of reasons, not the least of which are financial stringency and the onset of slower growth, pressure for modifications in tenure policies appears to be developing. It should be noted that the Association of American Colleges has recently issued guidelines for standards to be followed in connection with the dismissal of faculty members who must be laid off for reasons associated with financial stringency (84). We would urge that such standards be carefully observed, but some separations for lack of suitable employment will be necessary.

In addition, because of the need for flexibility, we believe that employment contracts should be negotiated and tenure granted on an institutionwide basis rather than in a particular field. Furthermore, in multicampus institutions, employment contracts and tenure should be on a multicampus rather than on a particular campus basis. As overall growth declines, the rates of growth of different campuses may well continue to vary considerably. Thus one of the ways of retaining flexibility in the use of faculty in multicampus institutions may well be through shifting faculty members from campuses with stationary or declining enrollments to campuses with similar functions but with rising enrollments. However, we believe that such shifts should occur on a voluntary basis if at all possible.

Faculty members, like persons in all other walks of life, age at different rates and in different ways. Some remain highly productive in research and stimulating in teaching well beyond the conventional retirement age of 65, whereas others show signs of failing to keep up with their fields or of some type of physical or psychological deterioration long before age 65.

During the 1950s and the greater part of the 1960s, when the job market for faculty members was tight, there was some tendency to raise the normal retirement age and to encourage flexible policies under which productive faculty members could be invited to continue teaching on a year-to-year basis beyond the compulsory retirement age, perhaps to age 70.[2] Under the joint influences of a looser job market for faculty members and financial stringency, there are beginning to be a few signs of a trend in the other direction. This tendency to adjust retirement policies to the state of the labor market may be found in other sectors of the economy as well — witness the trend toward raising or removing compulsory retirement provisions in pension plans of some of the large industrial unions in the early 1950s and a reverse tendency, accompanied by a trend toward generous early retirement provisions, in the late 1950s and early 1960s under the impact of a relatively high unemployment rate.

At the University of Chicago, the administration has resisted implementing a recommendation of a faculty committee to raise the compulsory retirement age from 65 to 68. It has also made it possible for faculty members to retire as early as age 58 on the basis of actuarially reduced benefits (86). At the University of Minnesota, a proposal to reduce the mandatory retirement age from 68 to 65 is under consideration (78).

The Commission believes that retirement policies should be as flexible as possible and that all institutions should have provisions permitting extension of the normal retirement age in the case of faculty members who continue to be valuable teachers. However, in all cases these extensions should be subject to regular review. On the other hand, we believe that there is a case for adopting pension formulas that would encourage optional early retirement in a period when institutions will be hiring fewer and fewer new faculty members. This would help to reduce the rise in the average age of faculty members that is bound to occur—a trend that will contribute to an increase in average salary levels within institutions. Encouraging optional early retirement would also have the advantage of making it possible for institutions to bring more young persons onto the faculty.

Between 1966 and 1970, the proportion of men beginning to receive annuities under Teachers Insurance and Annuity Association plans who were aged 60 to 64 increased from 8.7 to 10.8 percent of all beginning annuitants, while the corresponding proportion of

---

[2] In 1968, the great majority of four-year institutions of higher education had a normal retirement age of 65, but nearly all permitted extensions beyond the normal retirement age (85, p. 6).

women increased from 14.7 to 19.3 percent (87). Although some of these men and women may not have left the labor force altogether— some may have accepted teaching positions at other institutions— the data do seem to suggest something of a trend toward earlier retirement. The TIAA is currently studying the question of financial incentives that might encourage and facilitate the voluntary early retirement of faculty members. An important aspect of such a study should be an attempt to develop data on the characteristics of faculty members who retire early and their reasons for opting for an early retirement.

Another important question concerns the costs of a plan which would encourage optional early retirement—presumably through a pension formula that would involve less than full actuarial reduction of early retirement benefits—as compared with the savings that would accrue by replacing early retirees with young faculty members at considerably lower salaries. A study of the comparative early retirement experience under academic pension plans with differing benefit formulas affecting early retirement should provide some basis for estimating the impact of more generous early retirement schemes on the rate of early retirement. Several studies have shown that the propensity to retire tends to vary directly with the ratio of prospective retirement benefits to earnings before retirement, although it is also strongly influenced by health status and personality variabilities. But the income factor is closely interrelated with health status—aging persons who are in poor health nevertheless tend to continue to work if they cannot look forward to an adequate retirement income (88, 89, and 90). It seems highly probable that the trend toward earlier retirement of faculty members covered under TIAA plans may be largely attributable to the liberalization of these pension plans in recent decades.

We recommend that campuses consider the following special policies for increasing their flexibility to adjust to a period of a declining rate of growth:

- Recapturing certain vacated positions for central reassignment, as recommended earlier
- Hiring temporary and part-time faculty members
- Providing that tenure does not necessarily apply only to the specific original assignment of specialized field and location

- Employing persons with subject-matter flexibility, as made easier in the training for the Doctor of Arts degree, and by encouraging persons to shift fields where this is desirable and possible

- Providing opportunities for early retirements on a full-time or part-time basis

11. The Planning and Control of Capital Costs

Long-range planning of capital expenditures has become relatively commonplace in higher education, but there is still much room for improvement in this aspect of educational planning. Where a highly selective private university or college is involved, the future behavior of enrollment is a matter of institutional policy, whereas less-selective private institutions that are having difficulty maintaining their enrollments face more complex problems in planning future capital expenditures. However, the most complex problems face large state systems, especially in states such as California that have been and again may be characterized by heavy in-migration. Recently estimates of future enrollment growth at the University of California have been revised downward quite substantially, in large part as a result of the fact that the rate of net in-migration to the state has been declining. This illustrates the need for continued revision of long-range plans for capital expenditures.

Another weakness of long-range planning in many instances has been the failure to allow for the future impact of capital expansion on maintenance costs. As suggested in Section 1, one of the reasons for the financial difficulties that developed at the end of the 1960s was the heavy increase in maintenance costs that resulted from the large building programs that characterized the greater part of the decade. Furthermore, plans for financing the increase in debt service that tends to accompany capital expansion were probably based in many instances on the assumption that the institution's total income would continue to grow at the same annual average rate that had prevailed in the recent past. As Jenny and Wynn pointed out in their study of 48 liberal arts colleges, "ranging from rich to not so rich":

. . . plant expansion has produced a major future and probably accelerating expenditure escalation for plant maintenance, repairs, and replacement;

119

this has been built into the system for years to come, and we find very scant evidence that . . . this expense problem is being anticipated (47, p. 45).

Recently a consolidated agency concerned with all construction in higher education, the Facilities Engineering and Construction Agency, was created within the U.S. Department of Health, Education and Welfare. One of its major objectives is to bring about more efficient management, planning, and construction methods. "Life-cycle" costs of new buildings will be advocated as more effective than the use of initial costs in decision making. In other words, long-term operating, maintenance, and replacement costs will become as important in planning the financing of new construction as initial construction outlays (91).

Another problem stems from the rigid separation of capital and operating budgets, especially in large public systems. When plans for capital expansion are revised, because, for example, it is found that dormitory living has become less popular with students, it would be desirable to be able to shift accumulated funds from the capital budget to the operating budget to meet critical operating needs. Often there are obstacles to accomplishing this—funds may have been raised for the specific purpose of building dormitories or the plans may have called for raising the funds through a bond issue. Nevertheless, there would be advantages in adopting the principle of a consolidated capital and operating budget, so that funds could be shifted between capital and operating allocations at the discretion of the board of trustees.

The Commission recommends (1) that long-range plans for capital expansion be continually revised to meet changing circumstances, (2) that adequate allowance be made for meeting increased debt service and maintenance costs on the basis of several alternative and relatively conservative estimates of the behavior of future income, and (3) that capital and operating budgets be consolidated (with the capital budget converted to a rental cost basis), so that shifts can be made from one allocation to the other at the discretion of the board of trustees.

We have already suggested the desirability of including rental charges for the use of equipment in departmental budgets rather than including the capital cost of new equipment. For much the same reasons, we believe that departments, research units, and other users of space, such as libraries, should have budgets in which rental charges, representing total user costs, are included. This procedure would have several advantages. In defending requests for new FTE positions in its budget for example, the department would also have to request additional funds to cover rental charges for any additional office space that would be required, along with added classroom space that would be needed if the new FTE positions were to be associated with additional courses. This would have the effect of encouraging the department to use its space as economically as possible and would probably also result in more equitable allocation of space among departments and other users.

Application of this principle would also help to ensure that analyses of the financial feasibility of new buildings would include studies of the costs of debt service, maintenance, and depreciation, because adoption of the principle should be accompanied by the requirement that every plan for financing capital expansion also include a plan for financing the additions to departmental budgets that would be required to meet their added rental charges.

A general adoption of this principle of budgeting space should facilitate efforts to include rental charges in research grants and contracts financed by extramural funds, whenever a research project requires substantial additional space. Groups reviewing budgets should be able to see the total cost, not just the partial cost, of the endeavor as against the total output.

The Commission recommends that institutions of higher education develop plans for gradually shifting to a practice of requiring budgets of departments and other units to include a rental charge for the space they occupy and the equipment they use.

The move toward acceleration and integration of degree programs that is now under way will have a much greater effect, proportionally, on capital costs than on operating costs. As we pointed out above, a shift to a three-year B.A., for example, would save about 10 to 15 percent on undergraduate operating expenditures, after allowing for a probable decrease in attrition and for the fact that some students would require more than three years to complete the program. But it would probably save close to one-third on construction expenditures designed to accommodate increased undergraduate enrollment, on the assumption that a modest amount of increased enrollment could be absorbed without new construction.

If we consider the wide variety of developments discussed above that are now underway for acceleration and integration of degree programs, we must conclude that, if these trends continue, the potential for saving in construction costs will be very great.

Requirements for construction expenditures in the 1970s will also be reduced if students who would otherwise have enrolled in conventional colleges and universities decide to enroll instead in open universities or other nontraditional study programs. This consideration underscores the need for constant review at the state and federal levels of the impact of such programs and for modification of projections of enrollment at conventional institutions if these new programs tend to draw students away from conventional colleges and universities on a substantial scale.

The Commission recommends that all capital investment plans give full advance consideration to the possible impact of accelerated degree programs.

In recent years there has been growing interest in year-round operation as a means of accommodating more students without incurring additional capital costs—or, to put it slightly differently, as a means of achieving more efficient utilization of space. The saving in capital costs can be appreciable, but whether there will be overall net savings depends on whether increases in operating costs do or do not exceed savings in capital costs. The probability that savings in capital costs will exceed increases in operating costs may be high, other things being equal, when a campus or a state system is anticipating rapid increases in enrollment, but there are also many other influences at work, as accumulating experience at individual institutions suggests. The argument for year-round operation is particularly strong in the case of residence halls which may not otherwise be financially viable standing vacant a quarter of the time.

Several private institutions have adopted plans for year-round operation recently, which are working well or give promise of working well. In 1964, Beloit College began operating on a plan which combined year-round operation with provision for alternating campus and off-campus experiences for "middleclassmen." The plan has since been somewhat modified to make it more flexible than the earlier scheme. Students may complete their entire program for the B.A. in three to five years, and after successful completion of seven to nine (credit) terms on campus. All terms are

15 weeks in length, and there are 12 terms in all, extending over nearly four full calendar years. The fall term runs from early September to just before Christmas; the winter term from early January until mid-April; and the spring term from about May 1 through the first week of August. During his first three terms, the student is an "underclassman" and is encouraged to participate in on-campus studies. Under the normal program, the student is a "middleclassman" during the next five terms, which consist of one field term, two vacation terms, and two terms on campus. The field term is required and consists of service or research off the campus and away from home, which is designed to be relevant to the student's educational goals. The vacation terms are optional, but may also consist of work that is relevant to the student's academic interests or may consist of travel. Alternatively, the student can speed up his academic program by eliminating the vacation terms. Normally, a student is an "upperclassman" pursuing study on campus during his last three terms. The plan was originally designed to permit a 50 percent increase in enrollment (92 and 93).[1]

Colgate University has recently approved a plan for year-round operation, which, like Beloit's plan, is also designed to provide more flexible and varied off-campus and on-campus experience. Students would be required to attend school for one summer and could spend the fall or spring term away from Colgate in lieu of a summer vacation. This scheme would permit the addition of 300 students to the present enrollment of 2,200 without new housing. A plan recently endorsed at Dartmouth College provides for year-round operation and the admission of women. The new 12-month academic year would be divided into four terms, with students allowed to select any combination of terms, provided that they attend at least one summer session in four years of college.

Clearly, economical operation a year-round program in a private college will be facilitated if it is combined with enrollment increases which can be absorbed at marginal costs that are below current tuition charges. Moreover, each of the plans discussed above involves some degree of compulsory attendance by students in the summer—they are not free to opt out of the year-round plan. Year-round operation in a heavily subsidized public program of

---

[1] Although Beloit was classified as "in financial difficulty" in the Cheit study (5), there is no indication that year-round operation was responsible, and the economies now underway do not involve modification of this unusual calendar (94).

higher education presents greater difficulties, as the experience of the Berkeley campus of the University of California illustrates.

In 1967, Berkeley replaced its traditional series of two six-week summer sessions by a summer quarter designed to enroll its regular students. It was estimated that the program would achieve economical operation if enrollment in the summer quarter amounted to 40 percent of average enrollment in the other quarters. However, summer quarter enrollment amounted to only 26 percent of regular enrollment in the first year of operation, and, although its enrollment gradually increased in the following years, it never attained the target level. Meanwhile, it was found that an additional quarter could not simply be superimposed upon the academic calendar without some expansion of faculty, resources, and facilities. But the critical problem, after several years of operation, turned out to be the unwillingness of the state government to appropriate the funds needed to subsidize the operating expenses of the summer quarter. The Regents reluctantly resolved that if a choice had to be made between allocating the budget to the regular three quarters or to the summer quarter, the three quarters should have first priority on operating funds. In 1970, both the Berkeley campus and the Los Angeles campus, which had had a similar experience with summer quarters, went back to the traditional summer sessions, which were fully funded by student fees, and which catered to such groups as school teachers desiring to improve their credentials (95). However, a task force is continuing to investigate alternative ways of achieving year-round operation.

The Commission recommends that institutions of higher education carefully consider programs of year-round operation, but also recognize that the conditions that determine whether net savings will be achieved through year-round operation are complex and require careful study and planning.

The literature on productivity in higher education includes extensive discussions of effective utilization of space, but the issues are more complex than some authors imply, and longstanding attempts to impose standards for classroom utilization in California have not been fully successful, partly because the standards have been unrealistically high (96, pp. 92–95). However, another reason for the lack of success is illustrated by the experience of the Santa Barbara campus during a period of rapidly rising enrollment from

1963 to 1967, when classroom space was inadequate and attempts were made to "stretch" its use by requiring every student to take either an evening or a Saturday class. An analysis of this experience indicated that "the upper limit on evening and Saturday class size (with any significant number of those classes) is about 75 percent of the daytime size, and very probably less" (97, pp. 391–392). Because average registration in evening and Saturday classes was lower than in Monday to Friday daytime classes, the marginal teaching cost of these evening and Saturday classes was relatively high.

More generally, the traditional view of space utilization can be misleading because it focuses on capital costs only and fails to take account of the fact that attempts to increase the average number of weekly hours of classroom utilization "may also result in smaller classes with teaching cost increases which will completely offset the space-cost savings in a surprisingly short time" (ibid., p. 385). Furthermore, an Illinois study showed that classroom space, on which attention has chiefly been centered, represented only about 8 percent of total nonresidential square footage, on the average, in a sample of 34 institutions of varied types. The percentage tended to vary inversely with the size of the institution, because the larger institutions tended to have relatively more graduate students, with relatively greater needs for nonclassroom space, and programs in engineering and agriculture with needs for relatively large amounts of laboratory space (98).

Thus, we would conclude that although analyses of space utilization are an indispensable aspect of long-range capital planning, attempts to develop standards for space utilization should take full account of the complexities of the problem and of the need to consider operating costs as well as capital costs. Intra- as well as interinstitutional studies can be most helpful.

The Commission recommends careful study of space utilization standards and their reasonable application.

12. Other Avenues to Effective Use of Resources

1. CONSORTIA AND INTERINSTITUTIONAL COOPERATION

Significant economies can be achieved through consortium agreements and other forms of interinstitutional cooperation, particularly in graduate education. Specialized types of expertise need not be represented on the faculty of every institution belonging to the consortium if students can sign up for courses in any of the member institutions. Agreements can be worked out among the libraries of member institutions to achieve a division of labor in the development of specialized collections, and computer facilities can be shared.

The consortium movement grew rapidly in the United States in the 1960s, but a good many of the consortia are paper arrangements with little significance in practice.[1] There is serious resistance in colleges and universities to any departure from the traditional goal of independent development of the resources of each institution.

Nevertheless, the number of effective consortia is increasing, and in the last few years financial stringency has led institutions to seek forms of cooperation that probably would not otherwise have developed. The Atlanta University Center and the Claremont Colleges—formal federations rather than consortia—have a long history of sharing of resources that dates from the 1920s. Bryn Mawr College and Haverford College have a very active program of cross-registration for courses, while Bryn Mawr graduate students have long taken some of their courses at the University of Pennsylvania.

A particularly interesting example of an effective consortium of neighboring institutions is the Connecticut River Valley group in Massachusetts, including Amherst, Mount Holyoke, Smith, the

[1] A more extensive discussion of federations and consortia was included in the Commission's report, *New Students and New Places* (1971).

127

University of Massachusetts, and Hampshire College (founded under the sponsorship of the other four institutions). A bus circulates hourly, all day and into the night, among the campuses, and no campus is more than 20 minutes from another. According to President Thomas C. Mendenhall of Smith College, a joint deposit library is a source of great savings, particularly in the collection of learned periodicals (99).

A significant recent development that may have important long-run consequences is the active interinstitutional cooperation of private institutions on a statewide basis to sponsor studies of their financial problems and seek ways of meeting them. A 1971 report prepared for the Association of Independent Colleges and Universities of Ohio, for example, recommended that the state of Ohio make increased use of a policy of entering into contracts for educational services from private institutions at less cost to the taxpayer than would be involved in expanding similar programs in existing or new public institutions. Also suggested was a program under which the state of Ohio would purchase, through an appropriate state agency, such equipment as laboratory materials and library books for loan to private institutions of higher education, thereby achieving economies through large-scale purchasing power (100, pp. 7–8). In the fall of 1971, the New York State Board of Regents established a council of college and university leaders to develop a master plan for joint development of public and private higher education in New York City, while the State University of New York announced a major reorganization involving division of its 72 campuses into eight regions that would carry out academic and other programs on a sectional basis. One of the purposes of the reorganization was to bring about increased collaboration between the SUNY campuses and private institutions in each region. It was reported that both of these developments could lead to "cross-registration" of students, faculty exchanges, consolidation of expensive graduate programs in fields of limited demand, joint adult education and community service activities, and shared library collections, computer facilities and administrative services (101).

The Commission recommends the development and strengthening of consortia in higher education. It also welcomes developments that are occurring in several states in the direction of increased cooperation and sharing of facilities by public and private institutions of higher education, and urges that such collaboration be considered in all states.

2. MANAGE-
MENT
DEVELOPMENT

Increased emphasis on efforts to achieve more effective use of resources in institutions of higher education must be accompanied by increased concern with management development. However, management development programs as exemplified in private industry cannot be applied in the same manner in higher education.

In the first place, there is a strong tradition in higher education that presidents, chancellors, deans, and other top administrative officials should be drawn from the ranks of the faculty. We believe that this tradition is sound. College and university faculties tend to have confidence that an individual who has experienced the intellectual discipline of study for an advanced degree and who has engaged in scholarly teaching and research will be a more effective defender of academic standards and academic freedom than someone who is chosen because he has been a successful leader in business, government, or military service.

Moreover, in private industry it can safely be assumed that virtually every junior executive is anxious to rise through the management hierarchy. Thus the chief objective of a management development program is to identify employees who have the potential to become able top managers and see that they get appropriate training and varied experience within the firm. The situation in the academic world is quite different. Many professors have no desire to become top administrators, but are interested primarily in achieving distinction in their respective fields. Moreover, in recent years, episodes of campus unrest have created exceptional difficulties for many college or university presidents, and the tenure in office of top administrators has tended to decline. So it is scarcely surprising that many faculty members are likely to doubt the desirability of administrative advancement.

Another distinctive aspect of the academic world is the frequent policy of giving faculty members a strong voice in the selection of department chairmen—usually through a secret ballot, the results of which are forwarded to the administration. It has also been found advantageous, and is now a fairly common practice, to have rotating department charimanships and rotating deanships. Under such a policy, the term of a department chairman may be limited, for example, to five years or so. In some institutions, a dean is subject to confidential review by a faculty committee after a stated period of years.

Indefinite tenure for deans and department chairmen has been found to have many disadvantages. To be sure, when an exceptionally able administrator occupies one of these positions for many years it works well. But it has also been found on occasion to perpetuate an authoritarian style of leadership or to result in continuing loss of strength in a department, when an entrenched chairman became negligent about the job of recruiting able additions to his faculty. In addition, an able faculty member will be more likely to commit himself to serve as department chairman for, say, three to five years than for an indefinite period.

Acutally, these common practices in academia are likely to result in a fairly effective informal management development program. Faculty members tend to have good judgment as to which of their colleagues would make an effective department chairman, and a faculty member who has displayed exceptional qualities of leadership as a department chairman is likely to be called on at some stage to serve as a dean. It is scarcely necessary to add that an able dean may move on to become a chancellor or president, although boards of trustees often prefer to look outside their own institutions for a president, on the ground that a person who does not have close ties with the faculty will be in a better position to achieve policy changes.

Management development in the formal sense has generally been lacking in the academic world. In recent years, brief management seminars have been sponsored by foundations, professional groups, and some of the accrediting associations.[2] These are usually attended by persons who have already become administrators. Graduate courses on college and university management have also been introduced in some institutions, usually in schools of education.

Perhaps the most promising approach to more effective management in higher education, applicable primarily in large institutions, is the training and development of a middle-level administrative staff to assume some of the more day-to-day responsibilities of

[2] Information about several hundred programs of this type that have been held or are scheduled to be held in 1972 was recently published by the Academy for Educational Development (102).

department chairmen, deans, and other administrators (103, p. 26). In one large department in a major university, for example, an assistant to the chairman performs such functions as drafting letters in support of promotions, working out course and committee assignments with faculty members, administering a placement program for graduate students, and the like. In performing all these functions, he relieves not only the chairman but also other members of the department of time-consuming duties which they formerly performed. He has a master's degree in his field—probably a more or less essential prerequisite for some of his functions.

Similar assistants can provide valuable services to deans and to top administrators. They need not be as highly educated as faculty members, and they can acquire increasing expertise in their jobs over the years. Thus they can provide helpful advice to each new department chairman or other administrator as he assumes office.

Furthermore, assistants to deans and chief campus administrators can be chosen from the ranks of those who have successfully served as assistants to department chairmen and in that capacity have learned a good deal about the administration of the institution.

The development of such a core of middle managers would also have the advantage of providing a kind of continuity in the administration of an institution which is often lacking in higher education— not so much with respect to major policy issues, as with respect to a host of minor administrative policies and practices which need to be handled efficiently and consistently. Furthermore, since middle-management positions would be long-service career positions, large colleges and universities could expect to benefit from substantial investment in appropriate training for such staff members.

The savings would take the form partly of more effective use of high-priced faculty time and partly of more efficient and consistent administrative policies and practices. A department chairman who has the services of an able professional assistant should not need as much released time from teaching as he would in the absence of such assistance. In large departments, a vice chairman has often been appointed from the ranks of the faculty to assist the chairman, and he, too, has been granted released time from teaching. A department chairman who has the services of an able nonfaculty professional assistant should not need the assistance of a vice chairman, or of other faculty administrative assistance. In the example cited above, for instance, the placement of graduate students formerly required considerable time and attention from a faculty member who served as chairman of the placement committee.[3]

College and university presidents are frequently overworked and underassisted. It is particularly important that they have sufficient staff assistance of high quality. The emphasis on effective use of resources, by itself alone, places very heavy burdens on the central administration. The denial of able vice presidents to a president can be the most costly single mistake to be made.

Another important contribution that can be made by increased emphasis on management development is ensuring that adequate specialized training is available for those engaged in the many nonacademic aspects of administration, including accounting, finance, purchasing, and the maintenance of buildings and grounds.

The Commission recommends that increased emphasis should be placed on the development and training of a staff of middle managers who could assume many of the day-to-day functions of department chairmen, deans, and top administrators, thereby (1) reducing the amount of released faculty time required for administration; (2) providing more efficient and consistent administrative policies and practices; and (3) providing experienced and informed professional assistance to faculty members assuming new administrative responsibilities. There should likewise be emphasis on providing specialized training for nonacademic administrators.

The Commission also recommends that the president of the institution be given adequate assistance from a highly capable staff.

3. ADMINIS-TRATIVE COSTS
It goes without saying that the suggestions for increased emphasis on management development just discussed are designed to achieve economies as well as greater effectiveness in administration. But it may also be necessary for some institutions to conduct special studies of their administrative costs in an attempt to identify func-

[3] In large colleges and universities, there is usually a campus placement office to serve the placements needs of undergraduates and frequently, also, of candidates for master's degrees. At the Ph.D. stage, however, and especially in connection with placement in academic institutions, the recruiting department will want to communicate directly with the department in which the graduate student is being trained, and faculty members will inevitably be involved in providing written or oral recommendations, even though details of the placement program may be handled by a nonfaculty member.

tions or segments of the institution in which administrative costs may be excessive or in which administrative activities are poorly handled because of an inadequate or inefficient administrative staff.

As indicated in Section 3, administrative costs per FTE student can vary widely even among similar institutions. They also vary markedly by type and control of institution (Tables 3, 9, and 15, Appendix C). It should be noted that student services are included in these tables along with administrative costs. Average administrative costs per FTE student tend to be far higher in private universities and colleges than in their public counterparts. Interestingly, also, they do not differ appreciably between the more selective liberal arts colleges and the far more complex private universities. As would be expected, administrative costs of the less-selective liberal arts colleges are lower than those of the more-selective group and about the same as those of private two-year colleges. The lowest administrative costs among the private institutions are found in private comprehensive universities and colleges, but even among these institutions combined costs of administration and student services are substantially higher than in any of the public groups of institutions.

Undoubtedly an important factor in explaining the relatively high costs of administration and student services in private, as compared with public, institutions of higher education is the need of private institutions to devote far more attention to functions associated with the recruitment and selection of students. They also tend to place greater emphasis on alumni relations and on fund raising from alumni and other private sources. In view of the fact that there are economies of scale in the costs of administration and student services, the smaller average size of private institutions could help to explain their higher costs for these functions, but a careful study of our tables indicates that these costs tend to be consistently higher for private institutions in all size groups than in their public counterparts.

There is no question that the administrative structures of many institutions of higher education, especially research universities, tended to become more complex during the 1960s. The rapidly increasing flow of research funds was an important factor in this development, resulting in the creation of new research institutes with their administrative staffs, and in expansion of the functions of general campus administrators concerned with the negotiation and processing of research contracts and grants.

Administrative costs per FTE student rose from 1959–60 to 1967–68 at an annual average rate (6.3 percent) which exceeded the rate of increase of educational costs per FTE student (5.4 percent) during the same period. The relatively rapid growth of enrollment in public institutions, and especially in public two-year colleges, with their relatively low administrative costs, tended to hold down the overall rate of increase of administrative costs. And on a full-time equivalent basis, the annual average rate of increase of professional staff members engaged in administration and services from 1959–60 to 1969–70 (7.7 percent) slightly exceeded the rate of increase in professional instructional staff (7.5 percent) and was in turn slightly exceeded by the rate of increase in professional staff members engaged in organized research (8.2 percent). But the ratio of administrative staff members to students (on an FTE basis) tended to decline slightly in both four-year and two-year public institutions of higher education, as well as in private two-year institutions, whereas there was a reverse trend in private four-year institutions (11, pp. 22–30, and 68–73).

The rate of increase in administrative salaries (104, p. 29 and 105, p. 45) was not out of line with the rate of increase in faculty salaries (60, p. 85). Between 1959–60 and 1969–70, the median president's salary rose at an annual average rate of 6.5 percent, or only slightly more than the rate of increase in full professors' salaries (6.3 percent), while median salaries of other representative administrators (the dean of men and the dean or director of admissions) rose slightly less rapidly (5.4 percent per year) than average salaries of all faculty members (5.8 percent a year).

On the whole, then, the rise in administrative costs was reasonably comparable with the rise in faculty costs in the 1960s. And, like faculty expenses, these costs (on a per-student basis) are likely to rise less rapidly in the 1970s, because administrators tend to be drawn from the ranks of the faculty or are similarly educated professionals, whose salaries will be adversely affected by the deteriorating job market for Ph.D.'s. Nevertheless, it will be important for colleges and universities to conduct analyses of their administrative costs, particularly with a view to determining how they compare from one part of the institution to another and how they compare with those of other comparable institutions.

The Commission recommends that all institutions of higher education, especially those with relatively high administrative costs, conduct analyses of these costs with a view to identifying functions or parts of the institution in which these costs may be excessive or in which there is evidence of administrative inefficiency.

4. COMPUTER COSTS The use of computers has become indispensable to research in many fields, and knowledge of how to use computers has therefore become an essential aspect of graduate education in these fields. In recent years, courses in the use of computers and in elementary programming have also been made available for undergraduates in appropriate fields. Computerized instruction is still relatively rare, but it is being introduced in some institutions. And, of course, institutions of higher education, like other organizations, have long since begun to make extensive use of computers in the handling of payrolls, accounting, student records, and in the development of management information systems.

A study of costs at 10 major private universities showed that total computer expenditures in these institutions increased at an average annual rate of 41 percent from 1961–62 to 1965–66 (106). The proportion of these expenditures met by extramural sources of support declined from 68 percent in the former year to 42 percent in the latter, suggesting that the relative importance of computer expense in institutional management and in instruction, as compared with research, was rising.

Faced with these mounting expenditures, colleges and universities have sought various means of bringing computer expenditures under more effective control. In relatively small institutions, it is generally more economical, wherever feasible, to purchase computer services from a commercial organization or, in some cases, perhaps, from a nearby public agency or large academic organization. This is particularly true in view of the rapidity with which large-scale computers become obsolete. Even as large and heavily research-oriented an academic institution as the University of Chicago has found, upon investigation, that it would probably be more economical to contract for computer services commercially than to maintain its own computer facilities, and is contemplating a gradual shift (86). Perhaps even more striking is the fact that two such heavily research-oriented major universities as Harvard and the Massachusetts Institute of Technology are now sharing their computer facilities and finding that there are economies involved (107). Another principle being enforced at MIT is to make certain that full-cost charges are made for computer services used in research. This practice also tends to ensure that computer expense incurred by doctoral candidates is fully covered by outside sources of support, because most doctoral theses at MIT are prepared under the auspices of extramurally financed research projects.

Consistent with the general principles which were discussed above, we also believe that the full costs of computer expenditures in connection with instruction and departmental research should appear in departmental budgets and should not be subsidized from general institutional sources.

The Commission recommends that all institutions of higher education seek economies in computer expenditures by (1) contracting for computer services where this is found to be advantageous, (2) charging the full costs of computer services used in instruction and departmental research against departmental budgets, (3) charging the full costs of computer services used in extramurally financed research against the relevant research budgets, and (4) sharing computer facilities with nearby institutions of higher education where this appears to be a more advantageous solution than contracting out.

5. OVER-COMING MEDICAL AND DENTAL SCHOOL DEFICITS One of the sources of financial difficulty for some universities is the problem of medical and dental school deficits. According to Fein and Weber, the medical schools that have been facing the most serious financial difficulties are the weakly financed private schools that are heavily dependent on tuition as a source of income (108, p. 46). For example, all the Jesuit schools — Saint Louis, Georgetown, Creighton, Loyola-Stritch, and Marquette — have had to rely heavily on financial assistance from their parent universities.[4] Another group of medical schools in financial difficulty are the non-university-affiliated schools — Hahnemann, Jefferson, Women's Medical College, Chicago Medical School, and Meharry.

A recent report on financial distress in medical and dental schools, submitted to Congress by Secretary Elliot Richardson of the Department of Health, Education and Welfare, tends to confirm the Fein-Weber findings to some degree (109). For example, there tended to be a negative correlation between the receipt of a project grant ("financial distress") award and the amount of research funds received by the school from the federal government.

[4] Marquette University's medical school has recently been reorganized as the Medical College of Wisconsin at Milwaukee and is now receiving substantial financial support from the state of Wisconsin.

Despite the evidence that, in general, it is the weakly financed, non-research-oriented schools that have experienced the most serious financial difficulty, some of the strongest and most highly research-oriented medical schools in the nation have been experiencing sizable deficits in recent years.

For example, Johns Hopkins School of Medicine was reported in the spring of 1971 to account for $2 million of its parent university's overall deficit of $4.3 million. Part of the school's problem resulted from cutbacks in federal research grants, but a major factor was its location in a low-income inner city area, where its teaching hospital served many indigent patients for whom it was not adequately reimbursed under federal, state, and local medical assistance programs. According to its treasurer, D. Thomas Barnes, in 1970 the hospital provided $3.4 million worth of medical services for which it received no payment whatsoever (110). Other sources of the school's financial problems were reported to be the overhead costs of maintaining expensive facilities regardless of whether funds were available to use them, unionization of employees, and the rise in the cost of medical education.

According to Provost John T. Wilson, the University of Chicago's medical school has a similar problem of inadequate reimbursement for the care of indigent patients in its main teaching hospital, and the deficits so incurred are a drain on the parent university's funds.

Enactment of the Comprehensive Health Manpower Act of 1971 has meant that the nation's medical and dental schools are now receiving substantially increased financial support for their educational programs, but we do not believe the support will be adequate, or that it will permit the phasing out of "financial distress" grants, until the level of funding under the act is brought from its current 65 percent to 100 percent of authorized levels. In addition, it appears unlikely that medical and dental education will be adequately financed until there is a more general policy of state support of private medical and dental schools, along the lines earlier recommended by the Commission. In recent years, the number of states providing financial support to private medical schools has increased from three to nine, and these nine states include 26 of the 46 private medical schools.[5] In general, state support of medical and dental education is very uneven, and a recent report on state appropriations for teaching hospitals in public medical schools

---

[5] However, one of the nine is Maryland, which by the end of 1971 had authorized assistance to its only private medical school, Johns Hopkins, but had not yet appropriated funds for the purpose (109, p. 34).

showed extremely wide variations in the percentages of total operating budgets provided through state appropriations (111).

The Commission has suggested that a university health science center may find it advantageous to rely on agreements with affiliated hospitals, as in the case of the Harvard Medical School, rather than to own its own teaching hospital (112, p. 44). Although the administration of the health science center and of affiliated teaching hospitals must be closely coordinated, their objectives are not identical. The hospitals must be concerned primarily with patient care, while the health science center must be concerned with high quality professional education, research, and community service. The problems of administering a large university health science center are sufficiently complex without direct involvement in the administration of a teaching hospital. A recent article reported what is apparently an unprecedented problem of turnover among deans of medical schools (113). The problem was attributed to the enormous growth in the scope and complexity of these schools in the last decade. It may be no mere coincidence that all the deans mentioned as having recently resigned were in medical schools that owned their teaching hospitals. We have already suggested that there are advantages in appointing deans and department chairmen for specific, limited terms rather than for indefinite periods. This policy is especially desirable in connection with attracting an able faculty member to assume the arduous and complex responsibilities associated with the deanship of a large university health science center. In addition, there is a particularly strong case for the development of a core of middle managers in a health science center, to relieve the dean and other faculty members of the more routine administrative functions, as some medical schools are now doing.

However, the problem of deficits in teaching hospitals is not likely to be solved until we have developed a more adequate national system of financing health care. As the recent HEW report on financial distress put it:

Probably the single most important factor in achieving long-run financial stability for health science center operations will be the development of adequate sources and mechanisms of reimbursement for patient service activities (109, p. 118).

The Commission recommends that all universities with university health science centers seek to ensure that management of these centers is organized in such a way as to enable the centers to meet the greatly increased responsibilities they are now being asked to fulfill. Among the policies that are likely to contribute to effective management are (1) separate, but coordinated, administration of health science centers and teaching hospitals and, where feasible, reliance on agreements with affiliated hospitals rather than ownership of a teaching hospital, and (2) development of an able core of middle managers to assume responsibility for the more routine administrative functions.

6. AUXILIARY ENTERPRISES

For relatively small colleges and universities, particularly, there appear to be advantages in contracting out the operation of cafeteria services. In this way, they benefit from the large-scale purchasing power of private contractors who operate on a concession basis for a number of clients. In 1969–70, about one-half of all colleges and universities responding to an annual survey operated their own food service programs, while the other half had entered into arrangements with private contractors. Not surprisingly, contracting out tended to be more prevalent among private institutions, with their smaller average size, than among public institutions. In addition to those currently operating food services through private contractors, an additional 16 percent of all responding institutions reported that they were developing plans for such arrangements, and the majority of these had enrollments of less than 5,000 (114).

Provision of student housing through arrangements with private firms is less prevalent than the contracting out of food services, but there is a trend toward increasing use of this type of arrangement. In 1969–70, 33 percent of the public institutions and 22 percent of the private institutions responding to the same survey cited above reported that some of their students were accommodated in housing developed by private firms with college cooperation. This represented a significant increase over the previous year. Operation by a private firm need not necessarily interfere with efforts to provide a stimulating living environment for students that emphasizes faculty-student contacts, as in the Harvard and Yale "houses," which are now being emulated in other institutions.

Some of the most economical student housing is provided by student cooperatives, but the economies are achieved largely through requirements that all student members of the cooperative contribute a certain number of hours of work per week in food and room services. Similarly, economies can be achieved where there is extensive use of student help in institutionally operated dormitories.

Under the federal work-study program, student jobs of this type can be provided at relatively little expense to the institution.

For all institutions of higher education, total revenue from auxiliary enterprises exceeded total expenditures for their operation by $181 million in 1967–68 (60, pp. 92 and 96). However, there are some institutions that subsidize their auxiliary enterprises to some extent. This is especially true of some of the predominantly black colleges in the South, with their high proportion of low-income students.

The Commission believes that the charges of auxiliary enterprises should cover their costs and that students who cannot afford these charges should be assisted through student aid or jobs rather than through subsidized operation of auxiliary enterprises. Otherwise, students who can afford to pay full-cost charges will unnecessarily benefit from subsidies.

The Commission recommends that all colleges and universities seek maximum economies in the operation of auxiliary services. These may be achieved through (1) contracting out, especially in small colleges and universities, (2) the development of student cooperative housing, and (3) employing students in food and room service activities. Students should be charged for services on a full-cost basis, and those who cannot afford these charges should be assisted through student aid or jobs.

7. STUDENT-AID POLICIES
Throughout higher education, high priority is being given to efforts to provide adequate student aid—partly because of increased concern over equality of opportunity, and partly because the accelerated tuition increases necessitated by rising costs have tended to be accompanied by increases in student-aid expenditures to mitigate the adverse effects of tuition increases on low-income and lower-middle-income students. The role of increased student-aid expenditures in accounting for growing deficits, especially in private institutions of higher education, was discussed earlier.

Colleges and universities will continue to face serious difficulties in providing adequate student aid until federal student-aid expenditures are brought up to something approximating the levels that have been recommended by the Commission.[6] There is also a need for more widespread and liberal state government student-aid programs.

[6] See the Commission reports cited on p. 46.

However, in the meantime some institutions are finding that they can "stretch" their student-aid funds by placing relatively greater emphasis on loans and work opportunities as compared with scholarships and grants. For example, among the recommendations of the Princeton Priorities Committee for the fiscal year 1971–72 was a restructuring of student-aid policies to require students receiving combinations of grants and loans to accept larger amounts of their total aid package in the form of loans as compared with grants (58, pp. 85–101). Nondisadvantaged undergraduates were to be required to accept $500 in the form of loans in fiscal year 1971–72, with the amount required to be in the form of a loan gradually increasing to $1,000 by 1974–75. The increases were to be somewhat less for disadvantaged students.

Harvard University has recently announced a new long-term loan program for undergraduates and graduate students (115, p. 12). The program is designed to "ease the impact of increasing tuition and living costs in all parts of the University, and to provide repayment features contingent on a graduate's income." The new program will utilize the federal Guaranteed Insured Loan Program, but existing loan funds of the university will also be channeled into it.

A more pronounced innovation is Yale's deferred tuition plan.

The Commission recommends that colleges and universities seek maximum effectiveness in the allocation of student-aid funds through limiting aid given exclusively in the form of grants to the neediest and most disadvantaged students, while providing combinations of grants, loans, and work opportunities to less needy students.

8. FINANCING STUDENT SERVICES

During the postwar period, there has been a pronounced tendency for colleges and universities to increase the scope and variety of student services provided. Counseling and placement services have been introduced where they did not previously exist, student health services have been initiated or improved, and cultural centers have been established.

Financial stringency is leading many institutions to conduct thoroughgoing reviews of student services, often with particular reference to the question of whether and to what extent these services should be subsidized. Mounting costs of health care, in particular, have led to scrutiny of student health services. Decades ago, when private health insurance was nonexistent in the United

States and community hospital facilities were seriously inadequate, there was some tendency for large universities to establish their own student hospitals. Small institutions frequently maintained infirmaries for students with minor illnesses. With the expansion of private health insurance and improvement of community hospital facilities, the case for special student hospitals has been considerably weakened. This is particularly true in view of the growing complexity and high rate of obsolescence of modern hospital equipment.

One of the most thoroughgoing reviews of student services of which we are aware was conducted by the Commission on Effective Use of Resources at New York University. The Commission recommended, as a general principle, that student services with income possibilities should introduce fees or revise their fee structures in such a way as to cover half of their costs through fees. More specifically the Commission recommended, among other things, that (1) student placement services should be subject to fees which would contribute to their financial support, (2) health services at the Washington Square Campus should be limited to emergency and referral services and to maintaining a small infirmary for noncommuting students, (3) the administration investigate the possibility of negotiating an agreement with the Health Insurance Plan of Greater New York or an alternative private insurance plan, and (4) plans for establishing an FM radio station be dropped (55).

The Commission recommends that colleges and universities review their student services, with particular reference to reducing the extent of subsidization of these services where it seems justified. However, in view of the critical need for counseling services for disadvantaged students, the changes that are occurring in patterns of participation in higher education, and the complex shifts that are taking place in the labor market for college graduates, we believe that counseling services will need to be expanded rather than contracted in many colleges and universities.

13. The Management of Income and Endowment

In this report, we have placed major emphasis on the control of expenditures, rather than on efforts to increase income, as a major avenue to overcoming the problem of unbalanced budgets. The reason for this relative emphasis is the growing evidence that institutions of higher education will not be able to overcome their budgetary difficulties only by attempting to bring about an increase in their revenues that will be sufficient to meet rising costs. And yet, a program aimed at maximization of income should be an essential part of each institution's plan for achieving effective use of resources.

One of the chief reasons that efforts to increase income are not likely to solve the budgetary problems of institutions of higher education, especially private colleges and universities, is that tuition in private higher education has been rising more rapidly than per capita personal disposable income. This has also been true of tuition in public higher education in very recent years. As we noted above, the cost of education per FTE student has been rising more rapidly than the consumer price index, and both public and private institutions have tended to raise tuition more or less in accordance with increased costs, although this has been more consistently true of private than of public institutions.

Between 1967–68 and 1969–70, tuition increases occurred at an accelerated rate in both public and private institutions, exceeding the rate of increase in educational costs in the latter and, in addition, exceeding the rate of increase in per capita disposable income (see text table, p. 144). Most of the less-selective private colleges and universities recognize that they cannot go on increasing tuition at a rate that exceeds the rate of increase in public institutions without losing students, and yet, unless the rate of increase in educational costs can be brought down, they are likely to continue

| | Annual average rate of increase in | | | | |
| | Tuition and required fees | | Educational costs per FTE student | | Per capita personal disposable income (current dollars) |
	Public institutions	Private institutions	Public institutions	Private institutions	
1959-60 to 1963-64	3.8%	5.9%	2.2%	6.7%	3.6%
1963-64 to 1967-68	5.0	6.4	5.4	8.6	6.5
1967-68 to 1969-70	6.1	8.1	8.4	8.0	6.7
1959-60 to 1969-70	4.7	6.6	5.0	7.7	5.4

SOURCE: Adapted from U.S. Office of Education data and U.S. Bureau of Economic Analysis, Department of Commerce, data by the Carnegie Commission staff.

to be faced with a cost-income squeeze. Public institutions of higher education, in which tuition meets a far smaller proportion of educational costs per student, are less likely to be faced with a problem of losing students as a result of tuition increases, but are likely to face a cost-income squeeze as long as state appropriations for public higher education are as restrictive as they have been in the last few years.

It is interesting to note that, at least in part as a result of pressure from governors and state legislatures, tuition and required fees in public higher education rose more rapidly between 1967-68 and 1969-70 than in earlier years. In several states, including New York, Ohio, and Wisconsin, there have been recent proposals to levy full-cost tuition in public higher education, and to increase maximum student grants simultaneously, in order to improve the capacity of private institutions to compete with public institutions for students.[1]

Pressure to increase tuition for state residents in public institutions is likely to increase as a result of court decisions limiting the period of time required for legal residence in a state to not more than 30 days, along with the recent acquisition of adulthood by 18- to 20-year-olds. The combined effect of these two developments will be to make differentially higher (often much higher) tuition

[1] These issues will be considered in the Commission's forthcoming report, *Who Benefits and Who Should Pay in Higher Education?*, to be published by McGraw-Hill Book Company.

for students from out of state inapplicable in practice. The results will be especially significant in reducing total income from tuition unless in-state tuition is raised in major public universities that attract many out-of-state students, such as the University of California, the University of Michigan, and the University of Wisconsin.

2. EFFECTIVE STUDENT RECRUITMENT For the less-selective private colleges and universities, effective student recruitment programs have increasingly come to be recognized as an essential part of an effort to maintain income — indeed, in many cases, essential for survival. Highly selective colleges and universities do not need recruitment programs to maintain their enrollments, but tend to pursue recruitment policies aimed at such objectives as maintaining broad geographical distribution of their student bodies, attracting students with varied talents and leadership qualities along with academic ability, and in recent years recruiting able students from disadvantaged minority groups.

Maintaining effective contact with alumni through a strong alumni association is an important aspect of a recruitment program, as well as of fund-raising efforts. In strong alumni associations, local alumni groups often play a significant role in recruiting outstanding students and in raising funds for scholarships.

For most public colleges and universities, recruitment has been no problem in recent decades of rapid growth. Admissions offices have instead been concerned with maintaining equitable selection policies and with providing adequate information to secondary schools about their requirements and admissions policies. In recent years, also, public colleges and universities, along with their private counterparts, have placed increased emphasis on recruiting students from disadvantaged minority groups.

Although effective recruitment aimed merely at maintaining adequate enrollments has been the exception rather than the rule in public institutions of higher education, it has necessarily received some emphasis in relatively new public institutions and in those located in areas with relatively stationary or declining populations.

As we move toward a period when overall enrollment in higher education will be leveling off, there is little question that public institutions of higher education will need to devote increased attention to recruitment programs aimed at maintaining adequate enrollments. This will be particularly true of less-selective colleges located in areas characterized by net out-migration.

The size and organization of the recruitment staff is a matter that should be carefully considered by the administration. In discussing the two similar liberal arts colleges mentioned above, Robert Heller and Associates called attention to the fact that the higher-cost college had a recruitment staff of five persons, as contrasted with a recruitment staff of one person in the lower-cost college (12). The implication was that the recruitment staff in the higher-cost college may have been larger than necessary.

In an earlier report, the Commission has called attention to the desirability of coordinating recruitment programs aimed at increasing equality of opportunity for disadvantaged low-income and minority-group students among groups of colleges and universities on a regional basis.[2] Along with contributing to increased effectiveness of such recruitment programs, coordination would undoubtedly also result in economies.

The Commission recommends that all colleges and universities give careful attention to recruitment policies designed not only to maintain adequate enrollments but also to achieve such objectives as equality of opportunity, broad geographical distribution wherever feasible, and diversity in the student body. As we approach a period of stationary enrollment, many public institutions of higher education will need to place greater emphasis than they have in the past on recruitment programs aimed at maintaining adequate enrollments.

3. CASH BALANCES AND INVENTORIES   In recent years, management consulting firms and other financial experts have had occasion to call the attention of college and university administrators to the need to minimize cash balances held in checking accounts in order to maximize the interest yielded by the institution's liquid assets.

Similarly, inadequate management of inventories can be a factor in reducing income from liquid assets. Excessively large inventories of supplies or equipment tie up funds that could be yielding interest. On the other hand, inadequate inventories can sometimes result in the need for emergency purchases that cannot be made on the most economical basis. The management of inventories, especially in large institutions, should be handled by a purchasing division that includes staff members who have had training in business management.

[2] *A Chance to Learn: An Action Agenda for Equal Opportunity in Higher Education* (1970).

The Commission recommends that colleges and universities minimize cash balances held in checking accounts and make certain,
especially in large institutions, that purchasing functions and
inventory management are handled by persons with adequate
special training.

4. MANAGING ENDOWMENT FUNDS

Traditionally, colleges and universities have tended to be extremely
conservative in the investment and use of endowment funds. Stocks
have been regarded as risky, and many institutions have "played it
safe" by investing largely in bonds. This policy has typically been
accompanied by scrupulous avoidance of expenditure of any of the
principal of endowment funds.

Experts on the management of endowment funds now regard
such policies as excessively cautious and, contrary to the impression of many college and university administrators, not required
under the legal provisions governing the management of trust funds
in most states. Moreover, these policies have proved to be extremely
disadvantageous in inflationary periods. A 1969 report prepared
for the Ford Foundation, which has subsequently received widespread attention, stressed the unsatisfactory consequences of such
investment policies in the 1960s:

In a decade when the average price of common stocks has risen seven times
as fast as the cost of living, and dividends on common stocks have risen
three and a half times as fast, many endowments have been exceedingly
hard pressed even to keep abreast.

To some extent this has been the result of conscious choice on the part
of endowment fund managers. As a group they are conservative, and some
of them have insisted that their only duty is to safeguard the original dollar
value of the funds entrusted to their care (116, p. 5).

Subsequently, the Ford Foundation's Advisory Committee on
Endowment Management issued a report which concluded with a
lengthy set of recommendations (117). Among the most important
of these were: (1) endowment funds should be managed with a
view to maximizing the long-term total return, treating a dollar of
capital gain as equal to a dollar of income; (2) there should be a
specific plan for endowment support of operations, under which
each year an amount equal to 5 percent of the three-year moving
average of the market value of the fund is transferred from endowment to operating funds; (3) a careful legal review should be undertaken of all endowment funds that in the past have been classified

as restricted as to principal, with a view to reducing the total so classified to the minimum legally required; (4) all funds that may have to be converted into cash within perhaps five years should be removed from the endowment portfolio and invested separately in prime short-term obligations, but any decision to spend endowment should be taken by the trustees only after considering the opinion of the investment committee about the timeliness of the necessary security sales; and (5) trustees should not themselves attempt to manage their endowment portfolios, but should delegate that responsibility clearly and fully to an able professional portfolio manager who is selected on his past record and whose performance is regularly evaluated on the basis of comparisons with the investment performance of endowment funds of other colleges and of mutual funds.

These general principles of endowment management are being increasingly accepted, and we believe they are generally sound. There was occasional criticism of them in the period of falling stock market prices of 1969–70 on the ground that some endowment funds would have fared better with a larger proportion of bonds in such a period, but such criticism is, of course, inconsistent with the principle of maximization of the long-term total return.

The Commission recommends that colleges and universities should (1) aim to maximize long-term total return in the investment of endowment funds, (2) delegate responsibility for portfolio management to an able professional, and (3) generally follow modern principles of endowment management.

Endowment funds have, of course, been a much larger source of income, relatively, for well-established, selective, private universities and colleges than they have been for less-selective, poorly financed private institutions or for most public insitutions. And, although their relative importance as a source of income has tended to diminish over the years, as enrollment has risen, and other sources of income—especially federal aid—have increased in relative importance, they are still a highly significant source of income for many private institutions, and these institutions tend to pursue vigorous policies aimed at attracting additions to their endowment funds. We believe that, in general, public institutions of higher education have not placed as much emphasis as they might have on raising endowment funds. And yet, long-established public institutions — especially doctoral-granting institutions — have large alumni bodies whose capacity to contribute may be quite substantial.

Success in raising endowment funds, in this era of financial crisis in higher education, is likely to depend increasingly on linking endowment fund drives with long-term plans designed not only to make the institution financially more viable but also to bring about constructive change in its educational programs. An innovative plan of this sort has recently been announced by President Martin Meyerson in connection with the launching of an extensive fund-raising drive at the University of Pennsylvania (118).

The Commission recommends that public institutions of higher education, as well as private institutions, pursue systematic and vigorous policies aimed at attracting additions to their endowment funds.

14. Concluding Note

We have proposed that about $10 billion (in 1970–71 dollars) can be taken away from the prospective expenditures that would be made on higher education in 1980–81 if the trends of the 1960s were to be followed.

Half of this $10 billion can be found by creating shorter time options for students at all degree levels and by some reduction in the ranks of reluctant attenders.

Saving this half of the $10 billion spent by institutions of higher education would also save students and their parents large sums of money. Fewer years in college saves subsistence costs to students and also gives them a chance to earn more money in employment. We estimate that by taking advantage of the shorter time options we have proposed students can be saved an additional $1.5 billion to $2.5 billion if calculated on their subsistence costs in college beyond those that go through institutional accounts, and $4 billion to $8 billion if calculated on how much they might earn if gainfully employed.

The other half can be found by reducing the increase in cost per student per year (in constant dollars) from 3.4 percent to 2.4 percent. We note that the 2.4 percent is an average. Costs per student in research universities, for example, will need to continue to go up at a rate higher than the average as they build their library collections and their laboratory and other facilities to keep pace with the rapidly expanding frontiers of knowledge;[1] other types of institutions will need to increase costs per student less rapidly than the average.

This other half can be found as follows: *(a)* at least one-quarter by raising the average unweighted student-faculty ratio on a selective basis, campus by campus and department by department, from

---

[1] For an excellent discussion of the special costs of research universities see William G. Bowen, *The Economics of the Major Private Universities,* Carnegie Commission on Higher Education, Berkeley, Calif., 1968.

16 to 17; *(b)* at least one-quarter by calculating the lower rate of increase in real salaries per faculty member that is likely in the 1970s as compared with the 1960s; and *(c)* at least one-half by calculating the smaller increase in federal research funds if they rise at the same rate as the GNP in the 1970s as compared with the much faster rise in the 1960s. These three factors by themselves can supply most if not all this other half. Beyond these factors lie the many others discussed above.

We have strongly recommended not only a $10 billion reduction in prospective total costs but also a redistribution of 1 to 3 percent of existing funds each year to new and expanded endeavors. This requires savings on established programs. Thus the many other methods of reducing prospective expenditures, aside from the major ones just noted above, are of great importance in securing this 1 to 3 percent per year. Within the totality of all the available methods, there is great leeway for local choices in the course of seeking internal financing for this self-renewal.

About two-thirds of the total reductions we envisage will require hard policy choices within higher education (particularly on ac-celeration of degree programs and on adjustment of individual student-faculty ratios) and about one-third (particularly lower faculty-salary increases and lower rates of increases in federal research funds) respond to forces substantially outside the direct influence of higher education. The "liberating" of 1 to 3 percent of existing funds each year for new activities, however, will always require hard policy choices and actions within higher education. Thus the task we suggest that higher education undertake is an inherently very difficult one.

We are convinced that higher education in the United States can not only survive at a level of expenditures $10 billion a year less in 1980–81 than the trends in the 1960s would indicate but can, if wise actions are taken, demonstrate greater academic strength and more vitality a decade hence than it does in the early 1970s, particularly as it successfully seeks internal self-renewal. For this to be the situation, higher education must undertake initiative to make better use of its resources and not rely alone on the pressures and policies of society.

Our final recommendation is: That higher education should under-take internally the constructive actions necessary to get more effective use of resources and not wait for less constructive — and sometimes destructive — actions to be required because of external initiative.

Appendix A:
Statistical Tables

TABLE A-1 *Percentage change in state appropriations and operating budgets of state universities and land-grant colleges experiencing increases of less than 10 percent between 1970–71 and 1971–72*

Institution	Change in state appropriation	Institution	Change in operating budget
University of Hawaii	+9.65%	University of New Mexico	+9.86
University of Virginia	+9.15	University of Idaho	+9.66
Mississippi State University	+7.39	University of North Dakota	+9.55
Rutgers University	+7.06	University of Massachusetts	+9.52*
University of Massachusetts	+6.34	University of Utah	+9.24
University of Delaware	+5.53	University of Oregon	+9.20
Purdue University	+5.24	Rutgers University	+9.08
Louisiana State University	+5.19	Utah State University	+8.82
University of Idaho	+4.42	Oregon State University	+8.67
University of Iowa	+3.52	Clemson University	+7.93
University of South Dakota	+3.16	West Virginia University	+7.72
South Dakota State University	+3.00	University of Missouri	+7.48
State University of New York	+2.57	University of Hawaii	+7.12
University of Nebraska	+0.71	Michigan State University	+7.10
University of Vermont	+0.04	Florida A&M University	+6.86
Kansas State University	+0.01	Louisiana State University	+6.81
University of California	No change	Delaware State College	+6.59
University of Connecticut	No change	University of Rhode Island	+6.40
University of Kansas	No change	Mississippi State University	+6.26
Oregon State University	−0.08	University of Houston	+6.05
Washington State University	−0.31	University of Nebraska	+5.70
Montana State University	−0.48	University of California	+4.42
Delaware State College	−1.22	Purdue University	+4.27

TABLE A-1 *(continued)*

Institution	Change in state appropriation	Institution	Change in operating budget
University of Montana	−1.77	University of Montana	+4.01
Florida A&M University	−2.00	Iowa State University	+3.99
University of Illinois	−5.32	South Dakota State University	+1.92
University of Rhode Island	−5.64	University of Iowa	+0.67
University of Washington	−7.83	University of Oklahoma	+0.55
		State University of New York	+0.23
		The University of Connecticut	No change
		University of Illinois	−0.42
		Montana State University	−0.88
		Washington State University	−1.03
		Kansas State University	−2.67
		University of Washington	−3.68
		University of Kansas	−4.10

* Estimated.

SOURCE: National Association of State Universities and Land-Grant Colleges, *For Your Information,* Circular Number 169, October 28, 1971.

TABLE A-2 *Doctor of arts programs, established or in the planning stage, institutions of higher education, May 1971*

Established programs

Carnegie-Mellon University

English

Fine Arts (Music, Painting, Sculpture)

History

Mathematics

University of North Dakota

Biology

University of Northern Colorado

Botany

Chemistry

Geography

History

Mathematics

Physics

Zoology

University of Oregon

English

University of the Pacific

English Literature

Programs in the planning stage

Ball State University

Music   (1971)

Bowling Green State University

Biology   (1974)

English   (1973)

Speech   (1973)

Carnegie-Mellon University

Natural Sciences

Catholic University of America

TABLE A-2 *(continued)*

Claremont University Center		Physical Education	(1972)
Botany	(1971)	Ohio State University	
French	(1971)	Russian and Slavic	
Government	(1971)	Languages	(1972)
History (?)	(1971)	State University of New York at Albany	
Music (?)	(1971)	State University of New York at Binghamton	
Dartmouth College		Stephen F. Austin State University	
Drake University		Biology	(1971)
English	(1972)	English	(1971)
East Texas State University		History	(1971)
Biology	(1971)	Mathematics	(1971)
Chemistry	(1971)	Syracuse University	
English	(1971)	English	
Health and Physical Education	(1971)	Washington State University	
History	(1971)	Chemistry	(1971)
Industrial Education	(1971)	Mathematics	(1971)
Mathematics	(1971)	Speech	(1971)
Political Science	(1971)	University of Illinois at Urbana-Champaign	
Idaho State University		Economics	(1971 or 1972)
Biology	(1971)	University of Miami	
English	(1971)	University of Michigan	
Government	(1971)	University of Mississippi	
Mathematics	(1971)	Earth Science	(1973 or 1974)
Indiana State University		English	(1973)
History	(1971 or 1972)	Music	(1971)
Mathematics	(1972 or 1973)	Political Science	(1973 or 1974)
Lehigh University		University of North Dakota	
Economics	(1974)	Geology	
Political Science	(1974)	History	(1972)
Psychology	(1974)	University of Oregon	
Massachusetts Institute of Technology		German	
Middle Tennessee State University		Sciences	
English	(1972)	University of Washington	
History	(1972)		

SOURCE: Council of Graduates Schools in the United States, *CGS Newsletter,* vol. 3, no. 2 May 1971.

TABLE A-3 *Distribution of faculty members by formal classroom instruction hours per week, 1969, by type and control of institution*

Classroom hours per week	Research Universities I Public	Research Universities I Private	Research universities II and doctoral-granting universities I and II Public	Research universities II and doctoral-granting universities I and II Private	Comprehensive universities and colleges I and II Public	Comprehensive universities and colleges I and II Private	Liberal arts colleges I and II Public	Liberal arts colleges I and II Private	Two-year colleges Public	Two-year colleges Private
None	12.7	13.0	10.4	5.9	4.8	3.5	0.0	3.7	3.5	8.0
1–4	25.7	34.4	17.9	17.1	8.9	11.3	15.7	9.6	6.0	12.5
5–6	22.2	23.4	19.5	18.4	9.4	12.2	15.7	9.0	4.0	5.4
7–8	13.7	12.8	13.9	14.8	9.6	14.9	4.8	9.1	1.9	0.8
9–10	9.8	7.1	15.6	18.1	17.4	15.5	9.6	18.1	4.0	2.7
11–12	6.3	2.9	10.4	14.2	22.3	25.8	49.4	24.2	9.7	14.2
13–16	5.4	2.4	6.5	6.7	17.7	13.9	4.8	17.7	39.2	43.8
17–20	2.6	2.5	3.3	2.3	5.6	2.8	0.0	5.6	24.0	8.6
21 and over	1.6	1.5	2.5	2.5	4.3	0.1	0.0	2.0	7.7	4.0
Median classroom hours per week	6.0	5.2	7.3	8.2	11.0	10.0	11.2	11.0	15.1	13.6

SOURCE: Carnegie Commission Survey of Students and Faculty, 1969.

TABLE A-4 *Percentage of faculty members in public institutions of higher education who had served as paid consultants during the past two years, by type of employer and type of institution*

Type of employer	Research universities	Other doctoral-granting universities	Comprehensive universities and colleges	Liberal arts colleges†	Two-year colleges
No paid consulting	53.9%	57.8%	68.1%		75.0%
Local business, government, or schools	17.5	20.6	22.2		10.9
A national corporation	13.9	12.4	4.0		4.8
A nonprofit foundation	7.4	4.3	3.1		2.2
Federal or foreign government	13.1	11.2	4.5		0.7
A research project	8.6	8.4	5.4		2.8
Other	11.4	8.0	6.3		8.9
Total responses*	125.8	122.7	113.6		105.3

*Responses may add to more than 100 percent because some faculty members served as consultants for more than one type of employer.

† We have omitted data for public liberal arts colleges, because the number of respondents in this group was small.

SOURCE: Carnegie Commission Survey of Students and Faculty, 1969.

TABLE A-5 *Percentage of faculty members in private institutions of higher education who had served as paid consultants during the past two years, by type of employer and type of institution*

Type of employer	Type of institution				
	Research universities	Other doctoral-granting universities	Comprehensive universities and colleges	Liberal arts colleges	Two-year colleges
No paid consulting	43.5	56.6	66.4	74.5	83.5
Local business, government, or schools	22.6	23.9	19.1	13.0	12.7
A national corporation	20.1	11.2	7.4	2.9	7.5
A nonprofit foundation	13.4	7.3	4.2	3.0	0.0
Federal or foreign government	20.9	6.7	5.5	2.4	0.0
A research project	10.9	7.6	3.3	3.1	0.0
Other	14.1	8.6	12.1	7.6	3.8
Total responses*	145.5	121.9	118.0	106.5	107.5

*Responses may add to more than 100 percent because some faculty members served as consultants for more than one type of employer.

SOURCE: Carnegie Commission Survey of Students and Faculty, 1969.

TABLE A-6 *Distribution of institutions of higher education by student-faculty ratios,* by type and control of institution, 1967–68*

Ratios	Research universities		Other doctoral-granting universities		Comprehensive colleges and universities I		Comprehensive colleges and universities II	
	Public	Private	Public	Private	Public	Private	Public	Private
0–5.9		6.3						
6.0–7.9		31.2		5.6			1.2	
8.0–9.9		15.6	5.7	5.6		1.3	2.4	1.9
10.0–11.9	6.8	21.9		11.1	1.8	6.3		9.6
12.0–13.9	9.1	12.5	20.1	22.1	5.9	5.1	11.9	13.5
14.0–15.9	29.5	3.1	5.7	16.7	12.4	20.3	19.0	25.0
16.0–17.9	27.4	6.3	17.1	11.1	20.0	30.2	21.3	27.1
18.0–19.9	13.6		17.1	11.1	21.1	8.9	19.0	9.6
20.0–21.9	4.5		8.6	5.6	15.3	15.2	8.3	3.8
22.0–23.9	6.8	3.1	20.0	11.1	13.5	5.1	9.5	3.8
24.0–25.9	2.3		5.7		4.7	2.5	6.0	1.9
26.0–27.9					2.9	3.8		
28.0–29.9					1.8			
30.0 or more					0.6	1.3	1.2	3.8
TOTAL	100.0	100.0	100.0	100.0	100.0	100.0	100.0	100.0
Median	16.3	9.6	16.2	14.7	18.9	17.1	17.5	16.0
Number of institutions responding	44	32†	35	18	170	79	84	52

* Unweighted ratios of full-time equivalent students to full-time senior faculty.

† We have excluded two institutions with small student bodies and exceptionally low student-faculty ratios.

SOURCE: Adapted from U.S. Office of Education data by Carnegie Commission staff.

Appendix B: Note on PPBS and Institutional Research in Higher Education

In recent years, planning, programming, budgeting systems (PPBS) have frequently been recommended for use in institutions of higher education and are the subject of an extensive and growing literature. First developed in the U.S. Department of Defense under the leadership of Charles J. Hitch, then Assistant Secretary of Defense and now president of the University of California, PPBS are now used throughout the federal government and increasingly are being used in institutions of higher education, though not always in the fully developed form recommended by their proponents. However, as we noted in Section 3, President Hitch has become somewhat doubtful about the applicability of PPBS to higher education.

In their fully developed form, PPBS contemplate cost-benefit studies as a basis for decisions to expand or contract programs. Benefits should be related to the goals of the institution. Some analysts conceive of the benefits as the rates of return to investment in higher education in various occupations employing college graduates, and the Systems Research Group at the University of Toronto has developed measures of societal and private rates of return in occupations employing college graduates in Ontario as a basis for measuring benefits and the income redistribution effects of higher education. On the other hand, some analysts would argue that such rates of return do not adequately measure the social benefits of higher education and tell us very little about such often neglected impacts of institutions of higher education as their effect on the communities in which they are located. There is also a good deal of dispute over the extent to which differences in rates of return reflect actual differences in the marginal productivity of workers with varying amounts of education versus "imperfections" in the market. In other words, the benefits of higher education are not easy to measure, and, in practice, many institutions use various measures of outputs, such as degrees awarded by field, performance of their graduates on the Graduate Record Examination, and the like. Other institutions make no pretense of using measures of output, confining their departmental data-gathering to input measures, such as numbers of students enrolled.

Quite apart from these difficulties, there is some question as to whether the results of cost-benefit analyses should be permitted to determine the allocation of resources without reference to other considerations or values. Low-cost fields may come out relatively well in cost-benefit analyses, but this does not necessarily mean that they should be expanded at the expense of higher-cost fields.

At least one critic goes even further and argues that PPBS should be used only on an ad hoc and not on a continuous basis, on the grounds that no one really knows how to use them in any detail and that the main concepts of PPBS—cost-benefit and cost-effectiveness studies—are particularly useful in deciding if and how to begin new programs or enlarge, reduce, or eliminate old programs. It is in such situations that they should be used.

Even active proponents of PPBS sometimes recommend that such systems be introduced only very gradually, on the ground that the process of introducing a full-fledged PPBS procedure all at once is too complex and that an institution can adjust to the policy implications of such a system more effectively if it is introduced in a series of steps.

Along with the development of PPBS and management information systems, there has been a trend toward establishing offices of institutional research in recent years, and a recent survey indicated that slightly less than one-fourth of all institutions of higher education had offices of institutional research.

Although there is a growing literature on offices of institutional research, there is a good deal of disagreement about their functions. Just as there are several levels of management information, so offices of institutional research can conduct research on problems at various levels.

If one emphasizes research and views institutional research as a form of applied research, he may search for truth, understanding, predictability, and control, but avoid involvement in current operations. If one views institutional research as almost entirely a means of expediting the day-to-day operations, another kind of emphasis arises.

With the first view, an individual is likely to be conscious of the many shortcomings in operations in higher education but profoundly concerned with the lack of definite goals and the lack of clear-cut values in decision making. Hence he is generally concerned with studies that force administrators and faculty members to reexamine their goals as well as their practices. . . .

With the second view, an institutional researcher is likely to emphasize efficiency more than effectiveness. He is in danger of becoming so involved in operations and so identified with administration that he unconsciously accepts the limitations of the present scene (119, pp. 309–310).

The Comission believes that an office of institutional research will be more useful if it does not become too involved in problems of day-to-day operations and can devote at least part of its time and part of its staff to longer-range studies of how to achieve greater effectiveness in the use of resources. But we also believe that the office of institutional research should be directly involved in the decision-making process, particularly as it relates to the annual process of budget preparation and to decisions relating to the initiation, expansion, or cutting back of programs. If it is not involved in the decision-making process, it is likely to undertake types of research that are unrelated to problems facing the administration or are unrealistic in relation to what can actually be accomplished. These considerations suggest that, at least in large institutions, the office of institutional research should have part of its staff involved in the problems associated directly with the decision-making process and part of its staff engaged in longer-range studies. To combine both of these functions effectively, it probably should normally be within the office of the president.

Appendix C:
Economies of Scale

The Carnegie Commission staff has been conducting studies of economies of scale in institutions of higher education over the course of the last several years. Some of our analyses have been based on state or regional data, but the major portion of the work has been based on nationwide data for groups of institutions as classified by the Commission. Charts presenting some of these data were presented in an earlier report of the Commission, along with a preliminary discussion of our results.[1] The statistical tables included in this appendix should be studied in conjunction with the charts included in the earlier report.

Although there are differences in patterns of variation in the relationship between costs per FTE student and institutional size among types of institutions, public and private, there are certain generalizations emerging from our analysis that apply to all groups of institutions:

1   We have found educational and general expenditures (less expenditures for organized research) per FTE student to be a more satisfactory basic measure of educational costs for use in analysis of economies of scale than instructional and departmental expenditures per FTE student (used by some earlier investigators of economies of scale).[2] This is because there are

[1] *New Students and New Places,* 1971, pp. 68–81. A description of the Carnegie Commission classification of institutions is included in Appendix A of that report. The charts take the form of scatter diagrams with educational costs per FTE student on the vertical axis and FTE enrollment on the horizontal axis.

[2] Education and general expenditures (less expenses for organized research) include instruction and departmental research; extension and public service; libraries; general administration, general institutional expense, and student services; organized activities relating to educational departments; other sponsored programs; and all other educational and general expense. They do not include expenditures for auxiliary enterprises, student aid, or capital outlay from current funds (footnote continued on p. 164).

significant economies of scale in expenditures for administration and student services, plant maintenance and operation, and libraries, which are not reflected in expenditures for instruction and departmental research. We have also found that, for universities and for comprehensive universities and colleges, weighted educational cost per FTE student (with FTE graduate enrollment given a weight of three, as compared with a weight of one for FTE undergraduate enrollment) is a more satisfactory measure than unweighted cost per FTE student, for reasons that scarcely need elaboration in view of the relatively high costs of graduate education, discussed in Section 3. For liberal arts colleges, which typically have few graduate students, and for two-year colleges, which have no graduate students, we have used unweighted educational cost per FTE student.

2 Among all groups of institutions, exceptionally small colleges and universities tend to have relatively high costs. The cost per FTE student declines quite sharply as institutions increase in size from very small levels to moderate levels, after which the decline occurs at a diminishing rate or levels off. (What is meant by a moderate level varies among types of institutions, public and private.) Thus, when the data for individual institutions are plotted on a scatter diagram, with educational costs per FTE student measured on the vertical axis and FTE enrollment on the horizontal axis, the relationship between costs and enrollment tends to be best described by a fitted mathematical curve rather than by a straight line. But the plotted points are scattered very widely around the fitted line — there is great variation in costs per FTE student even among similar institutions of comparable size. Another way of expressing this point is that the simple negative correlation coefficient between cost per FTE student and FTE enrollment tends to be low, and the standard deviation tends to be high. This is not so much a reflection of little or no relationship between cost per student and enrollment, as of the fact that cost per student is influenced not only by enrollment but by a number of other variables as well, such as income per FTE student, student-faculty ratios, level of faculty salaries, and number of fields in which degrees are granted. In fact, as we have indicated in Section 3 — and this is especially true for universities, comprehensive universities and colleges, and community colleges — as institutions grow in size they tend to offer degrees in increasing numbers of fields, often adding expensive fields, such as sciences and engineering. Our data suggest that the variable, "number of fields," tends to exert its influence, at least to some degree, in the direction of increasing costs with rising enrollment, thereby acting as a counterforce to factors tending toward economies of scale.

(Footnote[2] continued)

In a recent study by Maynard (120), the measure used was educational expenditures less expenditures for organized research, other sponsored programs, and extension and public service. The latter two categories of expense tend to be relatively small in most institutions. Maynard's empirical analysis is largely based on data for public four-year colleges in selected states.

3   As a result of these complex and, to some extent, contradictory influences, we have found that a more significant and consistent inverse relationship between educational costs and enrollment emerges on the basis of multivariate analysis than on the basis of a simple analysis of the relationship between costs and enrollment. However, the data presented in Tables C-1 to C-19 shed a great deal of light on why this is true, i.e., on the factors influencing the relationship between costs and institutional size.

Universities   Unfortunately, many large multicampus institutions report financial data only for the entire system, not for individual campuses. For this reason, we have had to exclude them from our economies of scale data, in which the campus is the logical unit for analysis. This, along with the failure of some institutions to report financial data at all, presents a particularly serious problem in the case of public universities—we have data for only 44 campuses of public universities, whereas the Carnegie Commission classification includes 101 such campuses. Especially poorly represented are public university campuses with heavy emphasis on research, many of which are parts of multicampus institutions. For this reason, we are not presenting data for public universities by size class

TABLE C-1 *Educational expenditures* per FTE student (weighted and unweighted†) in research and doctoral-granting universities, by FTE enrollment, public and private, 1967–68*

FTE enrollment	Public		Private	
	Unweighted	*Weighted*	*Unweighted*	*Weighted*
0–2,999			4,437§	2,851§
3,000–4,999			3,814	2,624
5,000–7,499			3,882	2,605
7,500–9,999			2,789	2,019
10,000–14,999			3,694‡	2,384‡
15,000 and over			3,948‡	2,363‡
Mean	2,292	1,822	3,722	2,495
Number of institutions reporting	44		42	

* Includes educational and general expenditures minus organized (sponsored and other separately budgeted) research.

† Unweighted averages represent educational expenditures per FTE student; weighted averages represent educational expenditures divided by $3x + y$, where $x =$ FTE graduate enrollment, and $y =$ FTE undergraduate enrollment.

‡ Based on fewer than five cases. Detailed data for public universities are not presented because of the unavailability of data for many multicampus institutions.

§ Excludes two institutions with unusually high expenditures and small student bodies.

SOURCE: Adapted from U.S. Office of Education data (Higher Education General Information Survey) by Carnegie Commission staff.

in the tables in this appendix, although we do include the mean for each variable.

One of the charts presented in our earlier report[3] showed that, for all universities combined, educational expenditures per FTE student declined quite sharply until FTE enrollment reached about 5,000 and more gradually to about 15,000 FTE enrollment. In private universities, both weighted and unweighted educational costs per FTE student tend to decline significantly and consistently to about 10,000 FTE students and then to rise somewhat (Table C-1). However, private universities tend to be considerably smaller than public universities. Such data as we have for public universities (not shown) display a tendency for costs to decline to about 20,000 FTE students and then to rise slightly. But we do not regard the data for either private or public universities as providing conclusive evidence that their cost curves are U shaped—there are too few institutions represented in the largest size classes to provide conclusive evidence on this point. Even so, we cannot dismiss the evidence as necessarily meaningless. All that can be said is that there is a need for more satisfactory data that will include the cam-

[3] *New Students and New Places*, p. 70.

TABLE C-2
Instructional and departmental research expenditures per FTE student (weighted and unweighted*) in research and doctoral-granting universities, by FTE enrollment, public and private, 1967–68

FTE enrollment	Public		Private	
	Unweighted	*Weighted*	*Unweighted*	*Weighted*
0–2,999			2,274‡	1,455‡
3,000–4,999			1,760	1,209
5,000–7,499			1,417	936
7,500–9,999			1,316	965
10,000–14,999			2,052†	1,310†
15,000 and over			1,528†	928†
Mean	1,134	905		
Number of institutions reporting	44		42	

* Unweighted averages represent expenditures per FTE student; weighted averages represent expenditures divided by $3x + y$, where $x =$ FTE graduate enrollment, and $y =$ FTE undergraduate enrollment.

† Based on fewer than five cases. Detailed data for public universities are not presented because of the unavailability of data for many multicampus institutions.

‡ Excludes two institutions with unusually high expenditures and small student bodies.

SOURCE: Adapted from U.S. Office of Education data (Higher Education General Information Survey) by Carnegie Commission staff.

TABLE C-3 General administrative and general institutional expenditures plus student services, per FTE student (weighted and unweighted*) in research and doctoral-granting universities, by FTE enrollment, public and private, 1967–68		Public		Private	
	FTE enrollment	*Unweighted*	*Weighted*	*Unweighted*	*Weighted*
	0–2,999			1,169‡	746‡
	3,000–4,999			654	449
	5,000–7,499			646	424
	7,500–9,999			443	322
	10,000–14,999			506†	332†
	15,000 and over			466†	283†
	Mean	267	214	658	.438
	Number of institutions reporting		44		42

* Unweighted averages represent expenditures per FTE student; weighted averages represent expenditures divided by $3x + y$, where $x =$ FTE graduate enrollment, and $y =$ FTE undergraduate enrollment.

† Based on fewer than five cases. Detailed data for public universities are not presented because of the unavailability of data for many multicampus institutions.

‡ Excludes two institutions with unusually high expenditures and small student bodies.

SOURCE: Adapted from U.S. Office of Education data (Higher Education General Information survey) by Carnegie Commission staff.

puses of all the large multicampus universities before conclusions can be reached on this point.

When we look at Tables C-2 to C-5, we find that the components of cost represented display a pattern of variation for the private universities rather similar to the pattern observed in Table 1, except that administrative and student-service expenditures per weighted FTE student decline more consistently than the other cost components.

A final comment about this group of tables is that private universities tend to have higher mean costs in all the categories of cost represented than public universities, but the difference is narrowed when the averages are based on weighted FTE enrollment. This would be expected because of the higher ratio of graduate students in private than in public universities.[4] However, a considerably

[4] In 1969, 37.2 percent of the students in private universities and 21.5 percent of those in public universities were postbaccalaureate students (ibid., pp. 132–133). The considerably smaller percentages shown in Table C-6, though based on fall 1967 enrollment and not including professional enrollment (which at that time was included with undergraduate enrollment by OE), nevertheless suggests that research universities with relatively large proportions of graduate students are underrepresented in Table C-6. In 1970, graduate students represented 77 percent of postbaccalaureate enrollment.

TABLE C-4

Physical plant maintenance and operation expenditures per FTE student (weighted and unweighted*) in research and doctoral-granting universities, by FTE enrollment, public and private, 1967–68

FTE enrollment	Public Unweighted	Public Weighted	Private Unweighted	Private Weighted
0–2,999			572†	365†
3,000–4,999			424	286
5,000–7,499			334	209
7,500–9,999			315	230
10,000–14,999			380‡	244‡
15,000 and over			359‡	277‡
Mean	217	174	394	260
Number of institutions reporting	44		42	

* Unweighted averages represent expenditures per FTE student; weighted averages represent expenditures divided by $3x + y$, where $x =$ FTE graduate enrollment, and $y =$ FTE undergraduate enrollment.

† Based on fewer than five cases. Detailed data for public universities are not presented because of the unavailability of data for many multicampus institutions.

‡ Excludes two institutions with unusually high expenditures and small student bodies.

SOURCE: Adapted from U.S. Office of Education data (Higher Education General Information Survey) by Carnegie Commission staff.

TABLE C-6

Graduate students as a percentage of total enrollment, number of fields and FTE faculty per field in which a degree is offered, student-faculty ratios, and faculty salary data, in research and doctoral-granting universities, public and private, by FTE enrollment, 1967–68

FTE enrollment	Graduate student enrollment as a percentage of total enrollment Public	Graduate student enrollment as a percentage of total enrollment Private	Number of fields in which a degree is offered Public	Number of fields in which a degree is offered Private	Resident FTE faculty per field in which a degree is offered Public	Resident FTE faculty per field in which a degree is offered Private
0–2,999		22.0[a]		60[a]		5[a]
3,000–4,999		22.8		81		5
5,000–7,499		20.7		104		6
7,500–9,999		18.1		115		8
10,000–14,999		26.1[b]		152[b]		12[b]
15,000 and over		36.3[b]		202[b]		12[b]
Mean	12.3	22.6	143	107	6	7
Number of institutions reporting	41	38	41	38	41	38

[a] Excludes two institutions with unusually high expenditures and small student bodies.

[b] Based on fewer than five cases. Detailed data for public universities are not presented because of the unavailability of data for many multicampus institutions.

[c] Includes all faculty ranks of instructor and above, but not teaching assistants and other junior faculty.

[d] Weighted FTE enrollment is $3x + y$, where $x =$ FTE graduate enrollment, and $y =$ FTE undergraduate enrollment.

TABLE C-5
Library
expenses per
FTE student
(weighted and
unweighted*) in
research and
doctoral-
granting
universities,
by FTE
enrollment,
public and
private,
1967–68

FTE enrollment	Public Unweighted	Public Weighted	Private Unweighted	Private Weighted
0–2,999			236†	160†
3,000–4,999			198	136
5,000–7,499			158	105
7,500–9,999			126	92
10,000–14,999			347‡	214‡
15,000 and over			105‡	64‡
Mean	103	82	188	128
Number of institutions reporting	44		42	

*Unweighted averages represent expenditures per FTE student; weighted averages represent expenditures divided by $3x + y$, where $x =$ FTE graduate enrollment, and $y =$ FTE undergraduate enrollment.

† Excludes two institutions with unusually high expenditures and small student bodies.

‡ Based on fewer than five cases. Detailed data for public universities are not presented because of the unavailability of data for many multicampus institutions.

SOURCE: Adapted from U.S. Office of Education data (Higher Education General Information Survey) by Carnegie Commission staff.

FTE students per FTE faculty[c]		Weighted FTE students[d] per FTE faculty[c]		Mean full-time faculty salary[e]		Faculty salary expenditures[e] as a percentage of total educational and general expenditures[f]	
Public	Private	Public	Private	Public	Private	Public	Private
	8.5[a]		11.6[a]		$11,311[a]		28[a]
	12.0		16.9		11,841		29
	11.3		16.1		10,328		20
	12.4		16.6		11,345		22
	9.3[b]		14.4[b]		14,403[b]		23[b]
	9.0[b]		14.7[b]		11,828[b]		19[b]
16.9	11.2	21.0	15.4	10,754	11,563	24	24
41	38	41	38	41	38	41	38

[e] Includes all faculty ranks of instructor and above plus teaching assistants and other junior faculty.

[f] Educational and general expenditures minus organized (sponsored and other separately budgeted) research.

SOURCE: Adapted from U.S. Office of Education data (Higher Education General Information Survey) by Carnegie Commission staff.

TABLE C-7 Educational expenditures* per FTE student (weighted and unweighted†) in comprehensive universities and colleges, by FTE enrollment, public and private, 1967–68

FTE enrollment	Public Unweighted	Public Weighted	Private Unweighted	Private Weighted
0–599	2,576‡	2,576‡		
600–999	1,500	1,388	2,273‡	2,096‡
1,000–1,249	1,393	1,381	1,577	1,405
1,250–1,499	1,229	1,184	1,478	1,412
1,500–1,999	1,264	1,216	1,585	1,438
2,000–2,499	1,092	1,064	1,469	1,337
2,500–2,999	1,163	1,112	1,501	1,405
3,000–3,999	1,322	1,198	1,652	1,376
4,000–4,999	1,165	1,067	1,238	1,124
5,000–7,499	1,249	1,120		
5,000–9,999			1,464	1,197
7,500–9,999	1,214	1,092		
10,000–14,999	1,416	1,088		
15,000–19,999	1,536‡	1,208‡		
Mean	1,282	1,187	1,540	1,386
Number of institutions reporting	242		120	

*Includes educational and general expenditures minus organized (sponsored and other separately budgeted) research.

† Unweighted averages represent educational expenditures per FTE student; weighted averages represent educational expenditures divided by $3x + y$, where $x =$ FTE graduate enrollment, and $y =$ FTE undergraduate enrollment.

‡ Based on fewer than five cases.

SOURCE: Adapted from U.S. Office of Education data (Higher Education General Information Survey) by Carnegie Commission staff.

larger percentage of universities with heavy emphasis on research— and therefore with relatively high costs—is represented among the private than among the public universities. For this reason, the means in Tables C-1 to C-5 in this appendix probably overstate the cost differences between private and public universities. Comparisons based on the more detailed categories of universities in text Table 7 are more reliable.[5]

Some of the data in Table C-6 of this appendix are particularly interesting. In private universities, the number of fields in which a

[5] Many multicampus universities are also excluded from text Table 7, but we undertook a special check to determine whether inclusion of multicampus institutions would affect average costs of public universities with heavy emphasis on research appreciably and found that it changed average educational costs in this group very little.

degree is offered rises consistently with increasing enrollment. The pattern is similar among the public universities (data not shown). That this tendency serves as an important counterforce to economies of scale is strongly indicated. Most other variables in Table C-6 show less consistent variations with FTE enrollment, but the number of faculty members per field rises steadily with increasing size.

Comprehensive universities and colleges   In public comprehensive universities and colleges, weighted educational costs per FTE student tend to drop substantially to about 2,000 FTE students and then to level off (Table C-7). Weighted costs in private comprehensive universities and colleges decline between the lowest-size class represented and the next-size class, but then show little change to about 4,000 FTE enrollment, after which they drop off significantly. Instruction and departmental research expenditures display somewhat similar patterns of behavior (Table C-8).

TABLE C-8
Instructional and departmental research expenditures per FTE student (weighted and unweighted*) in comprehensive universities and colleges, by FTE enrollment, public and private, 1967–68

FTE enrollment	Public		Private	
	Unweighted	*Weighted*	*Unweighted*	*Weighted*
0–599	734†	734†		
600–999	808	750	995†	922†
1,000–1,249	748	742	807	732
1,250–1,499	664	643	667	638
1,500–1,999	678	655	747	681
2,000–2,499	603	587	726	663
2,500–2,999	663	633	731	684
3,000–3,999	767	696	847	706
4,000–4,999	713	653	620	563
5,000–7,499	733	657		
5,000–9,999			760	619
7,500–9,999	733	658		
10,000–14,999	844	649		
15,000–19,999	958†	749†		
Mean	721	666	746	672
Number of institutions reporting	242		120	

*Unweighted averages represent expenditures per FTE student; weighted averages represent expenditures divided by $3x + y$, where $x =$ FTE graduate enrollment, and $y =$ FTE undergraduate enrollment.

† Based on fewer than five cases.

SOURCE: Adapted from U.S. Office of Education data (Higher Education General Information Survey) by Carnegie Commission staff.

Of special interest is the rather steady and substantial decline in weighted administrative costs per FTE student in these institutions, public and private. Physical plant maintenance costs and library costs also show some tendency to decline, but less steadily and less substantially (Tables C-9, C-10, and C-11).

As in the case of the universities, the data for these institutions show a consistent tendency for the number of fields in which a degree is offered to rise with increasing enrollment, but even in the largest of these institutions the number of fields is considerably smaller than in the largest universities (Table C-12). There is also a tendency—not paralleled in our data for private universities, but displayed in such data as we have for public universities—for mean faculty salaries to rise with increasing size of the institution. Both of these tendencies—the increase in the number of fields and the

TABLE C-9 General administrative and general institutional expenditures plus student-services expenses, per FTE student (weighted and unweighted*) in comprehensive universities and colleges, by FTE enrollment, public and private, 1967–68		Public		Private	
	FTE enrollment	Unweighted	Weighted	Unweighted	Weighted
	0–599	588†	588†		
	600–999	247	227	614†	562†
	1,000–1,249	225	224	367	329
	1,250–1,499	222	212	427	405
	1,500–1,999	203	193	429	394
	2,000–2,499	187	182	371	337
	2,500–2,999	186	178	406	382
	3,000–3,999	188	169	387	318
	4,000–4,999	158	145	324	292
	5,000–7,499	182	164		
	5,000–9,999			304	247
	7,500–9,999	183	165		
	10,000–14,999	188	147		
	15,000–19,999	166†	131†		
	Mean	199	185	398	360
	Number of institutions reporting	242		120	

* Unweighted averages represent expenditures per FTE student; weighted averages represent expenditures divided by $3x + y$, where $x =$ FTE graduate enrollment, and $y =$ FTE undergraduate enrollment.

† Based on fewer than five cases.

SOURCE: Adapted from U.S. Office of Education data (Higher Education General Information Survey) by Carnegie Commission staff.

TABLE C-10
Physical plant
maintenance
and operation
expenditures per
FTE student
(weighted and
unweighted*) in
comprehensive
universities and
colleges, by
FTE enrollment,
public and
private, 1967–68

FTE enrollment	Public		Private	
	Unweighted	*Weighted*	*Unweighted*	*Weighted*
0–599	234†	234†		
600–999	219	201	263†	244†
1,000–1,249	208	207	174	159
1,250–1,499	167	160	186	179
1,500–1,999	183	175	185	169
2,000–2,499	146	143	200	182
2,500–2,999	132	126	163	152
3,000–3,999	160	145	204	168
4,000–4,999	110	158	126	115
5,000–7,499	135	121		
5,000–9,999			200	164
7,500–9,999	134	121		
10,000–14,999	132	105		
15,000–19,999	121†	96†		
Mean	155	144	187	168
Number of institutions reporting	242		120	

* Unweighted averages represent expenditures per FTE student; weighted averages represent expenditures divided by $3x + y$, where $x =$ FTE graduate enrollment, and $y =$ FTE undergraduate enrollment.

† Based on fewer than five cases.

SOURCE: Adapted from U.S. Office of Education data (Higher Education General Information Survey) by Carnegie Commission staff.

rise in faculty salaries—tend to offset forces making for economies of scale. On the other hand, weighted student-faculty ratios in both groups of comprehensive universities and colleges display a fairly consistent tendency to rise with increasing size—a factor clearly making for significant economies of scale.

Liberal arts colleges Educational costs per FTE student in private Liberal Arts Colleges I show no tendency to decline beyond about 600 FTE enrollment—in fact, they show something of a tendency to rise, although it is not very consistent (Table C-13). In private Liberal Arts Colleges II—except for the sharp drop between the two smallest size classes—educational costs tend to decline with increasing size only in a moderate and rather irregular fashion. The behavior of instructional and departmental research expenditures per FTE student is somewhat similar, but, if anything, more

TABLE C-11 Library expenses per FTE student		Public		Private	
(weighted and unweighted*) in	*FTE enrollment*	*Unweighted*	*Weighted*	*Unweighted*	*Weighted*
comprehensive	*0–599*	360†	360†		
universities and	*600–999*	108	97	109†	99†
colleges, by	*1,000–1,249*	101	100	83	75
FTE enrollment, public and	*1,250–1,499*	84	81	74	70
private, 1967–68	*1,500–1,999*	84	81	81	74
	2,000–2,499	65	63	82	74
	2,500–2,999	75	72	70	65
	3,000–3,999	82	74	100	82
	4,000–4,999	66	60	70	64
	5,000–7,499	64	57		
	5,000–9,999			74	60
	7,500–9,999	72	65		
	10,000–14,999	73	56		
	15,000–19,999	90†	70†		
	Mean	82	76	81	73
	Number of institutions reporting	242		120	

* Unweighted averages represent expenditures per FTE student; weighted averages represent expenditures divided by $3x + y$, where $x =$ FTE graduate enrollment, and $y =$ FTE undergraduate enrollment.

† Based on fewer than five cases.

SOURCE: Adapted from U.S. Office of Education data (Higher Education General Information Survey) by Carnegie Commission staff.

erratic (Table C-14). The decline in administrative expenditures per FTE student is considerably less consistent than we found in the case of comprehensive universities and colleges, and substantial only between the smallest size groups represented. As for physical plant maintenance costs, they show no significant tendency toward economies of scale in the more-selective liberal arts colleges, but rather significant declines in the lower ranges of the size distribution among the less-selective liberal arts colleges. Library costs display moderate and somewhat more consistent tendencies toward economies of scale in Liberal Arts Colleges II than in Liberal Arts Colleges I (Tables C-15, C-16, and C-17).

In these groups of institutions, also, the number of fields in which degrees are offered tends to increase with increasing size, but among the largest of these colleges the number of fields is much smaller than in universities and in comprehensive universities and colleges, as would be expected (Table C-18). However, if we compare the number of fields offered in the largest of these liberal arts colleges with the number in comparable size groups among comprehensive universities and colleges, we find very little difference. The data in Table C-12 tend to support the Commission's recommendation that a comprehensive university or college should have a minimum FTE enrollment of about 5,000—otherwise it is not likely to be very comprehensive.

Of considerable interest, also, is the decided tendency for average faculty salaries in Liberal Arts Colleges II to rise with increasing enrollment, whereas this is not the case among Liberal Arts Colleges I. Furthermore, in every size group faculty salaries are lower in the less-selective liberal arts colleges than in the more selective of these colleges, but the gap is particularly wide between the smallest groups of colleges. Undoubtedly related to this phenomenon is the tendency for faculty salaries to rise steadily as a percentage of educational expenditures in Liberal Arts Colleges II, and to represent a much smaller percentage of these expenditures in small colleges in the former group than in the latter group. On the other hand, student-faculty ratios tend to rise with increasing enrollment in both groups of colleges, but more steadily and sharply in Liberal Arts Colleges II than in Liberal Arts Colleges I.

One gets the distinct impression from these data that small Liberal Arts Colleges II are particularly subject to financial difficulty. In order to function as a traditional college, they must have a certain minimum-sized faculty, as well as certain minimum expenditures for administration, physical plant maintenance, and the library. But their costs per student are high, and they evidently are forced to offset these high unit costs at least partly by economizing on faculty salaries.[6]

Two-year colleges Turning to public two-year colleges, we note a tendency for their educational costs per FTE student to decline to

(Text continued on p. 182)

---

[6] It is true that a significant proportion of small Liberal Arts Colleges II are Catholic institutions, where faculty members belonging to religious orders serve without compensation, although these faculty members have tended to represent a declining proportion of the total faculty in many Catholic institutions in the last few decades. When these colleges report their expenditures to OE, they include "shadow" salaries for unpaid faculty members, but there may be some tendency to estimate these salaries on the low side.

TABLE C-12
Graduate students as a percentage of total enrollment, number of fields and FTE faculty per field in which a degree is offered, student-faculty ratios, and faculty salary data, in comprehensive universities and colleges, public and private, by FTE enrollment, 1967–68

FTE enrollment	Graduate student enrollment as a percentage of total enrollment		Number of fields in which a degree is offered		Resident FTE faculty per field in which a degree is offered§	
	Public	Private	Public	Private	Public	Private
0–599	2.7		22		2	
600–999		3.7*		24*		3*
1,000–1,499	1.0	4.0	27	34	3	3
1,500–1,999	2.5	4.6	33	38	3	3
2,000–2,499		5.0		42		4
2,000–2,999	1.7		38		4	
2,500–4,999		5.6		46		5
3,000–3,999	5.0		46		4	
4,000–4,999	4.6		55		5	
5,000–7,499	5.9		63		5	
5,000–9,999		11.6		69		5
7,500–9,999	5.3		78		6	
10,000–14,999	11.9*		79*		4*	
15,000–19,999	13.9*		102*		5*	
Mean	4.0	5.4	48	42	4	4
Number of institutions reporting	235	117	235	117	235	117

* Based on fewer than five cases.

† Weighted FTE enrollment is $3x + y$, where $x =$ FTE graduate enrollment, and $y =$ FTE undergraduate enrollment.

‡ Education and general expenditures minus organized (sponsored and other separately budgeted) research.

§ Includes all faculty ranks of instructor and above plus teaching assistants and other junior faculty.

¶ Includes all faculty ranks of instructor and above, but not teaching assistants and other junior faculty.

FTE students per FTE faculty¶		Weighted FTE students† per FTE faculty¶		Mean full-time faculty salary§		Faculty salary expenditures¶ as a percentage of total educational and general expenditures‡	
Public	Private	Public	Private	Public	Private	Public	Private
17.8		18.5		$ 9,542		35	
	12.0*		12.9*		$7,802*		22*
17.6	15.8	17.9	16.9	8,915	8,762	38	33
18.9	16.1	19.8	17.6	9,123	8,917	36	27
	16.4		17.9		8,920		30
19.7		20.4		8,972		39	
	17.3		19.1		9,352		29
20.0		22.1		9,586		37	
20.0		21.9		9,302		38	
21.4		23.6		9,671		37	
	19.2		23.5		9,808		29
19.9		22.0		9,618		38	
43.1*		48.8*		10,116*		30*	
37.7*		47.2*		10,569*		35*	
20.3	16.5	22.0	18.3	$ 9,369	$9,038	37	29
235	117	235	117	235	117	235	117

A note on the weighting of graduate enrollment: In all revelant tables, we have used a standard weight of 3 for graduate enrollment, except in Table 12, where a weight of 2 is used in the case of comprehensive universities and colleges. The latter weight is more accurate for graduate education primarily at the master's level, but the use of a weight of 3 does not yield very different results for these institutions.

SOURCE: Adapted from U.S. Office of Education data (Higher Education General Information Survey) by Carnegie Commission staff.

TABLE C-13
Educational expenditures* per FTE student (unweighted) in private liberal arts colleges, I and II, and public and private two-year colleges, by FTE enrollment, 1967–68

FTE enrollment	Private liberal arts colleges I	Private liberal arts colleges II	Two-year colleges	
			Public	Private
0–199		3,188	1,776	1,807
200–399		1,593	1,274	1,513
200–599	3,245			
400–599		1,625	984	1,269
600–799	2,150	1,551	1,056	1,007
800–999	2,320	1,518	990	1,334
1,000–1,249	2,515	1,478	939	971
1,250–1,499	2,347	1,453	989	
1,250–1,999				664
1,500–1,999	2,505	1,410	973	
2,000–2,499			1,043	
2,000–2,999		1,489		
2,000–3,999	2,648†			1,222†
2,500–2,999			977	
3,000–3,999			931	
4,000–4,999			1,014	
5,000–7,499			1,030	
7,500–19,999			817	
Mean	2,479	1,624	1,054	1,417
Number of institutions reporting	108	450	399	155

* Includes educational and general expenditures minus organized (sponsored and other separately budgeted) research.

† Based on fewer than five cases.

SOURCE: Adapted from U.S. Office of Education data (Higher Education General Information Survey) by Carnegie Commission staff.

TABLE C-14
Instructional and departmental research expenditures per FTE student (unweighted) in private liberal arts colleges, I and II, and public and private two-year colleges, by FTE enrollment, 1967–68

FTE enrollment	Private liberal arts colleges I	Private liberal arts colleges II	Two-year colleges Public	Two-year colleges Private
0–199		1,042	1,030	644
200–399		672	674	638
200–599	1,458			
400–599		733	562	491
600–799	995	705	619	439
800–999	1,059	714	571	537
1,000–1,249	1,246	692	559	421
1,250–1,499	1,115	709	529	
1,250–1,999				344
1,500–1,999	1,230	679	611	
2,000–2,499			613	
2,000–2,999		714		
2,000–3,999	1,167			465*
2,500–2,999			597	
3,000–3,999			606	
4,000–4,999			633	
5,000–7,499			637	
7,500–19,999			534	
Mean	1,170	724	615	563
Number of institutions reporting	108	450	399	155

*Based on fewer than five cases.

SOURCE: Adapted from U.S. Office of Education data (Higher Education General Information Survey) by Carnegie Commission staff.

	FTE enrollment	*Private liberal arts colleges I*	*Private liberal arts colleges II*	*Two-year colleges*	
				Public	*Private*
	0–199		925	371	591
	200–399		505	280	474
	200–599	1,403			
	400–599		475	182	442
	600–799	640	466	178	347
	800–999	629	435	189	395
	1,000–1,249	644	386	166	340
	1,250–1,499	614	408	201	
	1,250–1,999				170
	1,500–1,999	606	362	157	
	2,000–2,499			204	
	2,000–2,999		418		
	2,000–3,999	742*			494*
	2,500–2,999			164	
	4,000–4,999			209	
	5,000–7,499			178	
	7,500–19,999			112	
	Mean	677	469	195	464
	Number of institutions reporting	108	450	399	155

TABLE C-15 *General administrative and general institutional expenditures plus student-services expenditures, per FTE student (unweighted) in private liberal arts colleges, I and II, and public and private two-year colleges, by FTE enrollment, 1967–68*

*Based on fewer than five cases.

SOURCE: Adapted from U.S. Office of Education data (Higher Education General Information Survey) by Carnegie Commission staff.

TABLE C-16
Physical plant
maintenance
and operation
expenditures per
FTE student
(unweighted) in
private liberal
arts colleges, I
and II, and
public and
private two-year
colleges, by
FTE enrollment,
1967–68

FTE enrollment	Private liberal arts colleges I	Private liberal arts colleges II	Two-year colleges	
			Public	Private
0–199		525	227	303
200–399		233	120	237
200–599	371			
400–599		207	97	216
600–799	325	198	115	140
800–999	351	193	117	241
1,000–1,249	359	187	93	134
1,250–1,499	327	172	93	
1,250–1,999				84
1,500–1,999	317	180	113	
2,000–2,499			111	
2,000–2,999		185		
2,000–3,999	342*			155*
2,500–2,999			114	
3,000–3,999			125	
4,000–4,999			104	
5,000–7,499			118	
7,500–19,999			97	
Mean	340	215	114	227
Number of institutions reporting	108	450	399	155

*Based on fewer than five cases.

SOURCE: Adapted from U.S. Office of Education data (Higher Education General Information Survey) by Carnegie Commission staff.

TABLE C-17
Library
expenditures per
FTE student
(unweighted) in
private liberal
arts colleges, I
and II, and
public and
private two-year
colleges, by
FTE enrollment,
1967–68

FTE enrollment	Private liberal arts colleges I	Private liberal arts colleges II	Two-year colleges	
			Public	Private
0–199		176	112	197
200–399		119	83	75
200–599	188			
400–599		90	60	60
600–799	112	89	56	49
800–999	131	84	57	57
1,000–1,249	141	79	51	57
1,250–1,499	117	75	45	
1,250–1,999				28
1,500–1,999	128	78	39	
2,000–2,499			49	
2,000–2,999		62		
2,000–3,999	175*			32*
2,500–2,999			39	
3,000–3,999			34	
4,000–4,999			35	
5,000–7,499			28	
7,500–19,999			35	
Mean	134	92	55	95
Number of institutions reporting	108	450	399	155

* Based on fewer than five cases.
SOURCE: Adapted from U.S. Office of Education data (Higher Education General Information Survey) by Carnegie Commission staff.

about 1,000 to about 1,250 FTE enrollment and then to level off (Table C-13). When we analyzed the data for California public two-year colleges alone, we found a somewhat more persistent tendency for costs per FTE student to decline—to about 2,000 to 3,000 FTE enrollment. Nationwide data are affected by regional differences in costs, especially for faculty salaries. Many of the smaller public community colleges are in relatively small communities in the South and Midwest, where salaries tend to be relatively low. And the largest community colleges are in such cities as Los Angeles, Chicago, and New York, where faculty salary levels are high.

Educational costs per FTE student show a somewhat more persistent tendency to decline in private two-year colleges than in their public counterparts. Moreover, in some of the relatively small size groups, costs in the private colleges are considerably higher than in the public colleges, but the difference tends to disappear at about 1,000 FTE enrollment. The rise in the 2,000 to 3,999 group may well not be significant because of the very small number of private two-year colleges in this group. And, as we have noted for other groups of institutions, instructional and departmental research expenditures tend to vary in much the same manner as the broader measure of educational costs in both public and private two-year colleges, but mean instructional and departmental research costs are lower in the private than in the public colleges, whereas the reverse is true for educational and general expenditures (Table C-14). This reflects the fact that, throughout the size classes represented, instructional and departmental research expenditures tend to be lower in the private than in the public institutions. The relatively high overall educational expenditures in small private two-year colleges are explained by relatively high costs for other components—especially administration and plant maintenance—not for instruction (Tables C-15, C-16, and C-17).

In the two-year colleges, as in the other groups, the number of fields in which a degree is offered tends to rise with increasing size, but not to as great an extent in the private as in the public institutions (Table C-19). Faculty salaries also tend to rise with increasing enrollment in both groups of institutions, but in all the size groups in which they are represented, faculty salaries are distinctly lower in the private two-year colleges. Moreover, whereas faculty salaries represent a more or less constant proportion of educational expenditures in public community colleges in all size groups, we find here, as in the case of private Liberal Arts Colleges II, that faculty salaries rise as a relative proportion of costs with increasing size in private two-year colleges.

Once again, we note a tendency for student-faculty ratios to rise with increasing enrollment in both of these groups of institutions. The trend, though persistent, is somewhat erratic, especially among the private two-year colleges, and for the two groups with FTE enrollment ranging from 1,000 to 1,499, student-faculty ratios in these private institutions are considerably higher than in their public counterparts. Also noteworthy is the decline in student-faculty ratios in public two-year colleges in the two largest size groups.

TABLE C-18
Number of fields
and FTE faculty
per field in
which a degree
is offered,
student-faculty
ratios, and
faculty salary
data in private
liberal arts
colleges, I and
II, by FTE
enrollment,
1967–68

FTE enrollment	Number of fields in which a degree is offered		Resident FTE faculty per field in which a degree is offered†	
	I	II	I	II
0–199		10		1
200–399		16		2
200–599	22		2	
400–599		22		2
600–799	27	24	2	2
800–999	29	28	3	2
1,000–1,249	34	29	3	2
1,250–1,499	33	32	3	3
1,500–1,999	36	34	3	3
2,000–2,999		39		3
3,000–3,999	41*		5*	
Mean	31	24	3	2
Number of institutions reporting	106	437	106	437

* Based on fewer than five cases.

† Includes all faculty ranks of instructor and above plus teaching assistants and other junior faculty.

‡ Includes all faculty ranks of instructor and above, but not teaching assistants and other junior faculty.

§ Education and general expenditures minus organized (sponsored and other separately budgeted) research.

SOURCE: Adapted from U.S. Office of Education data (Higher Education General Information Survey) by Carnegie Commission staff.

This appears to be related to a sharp increase in the average number of faculty members per field in these two groups of large public community colleges, as compared with smaller institutions.

These data strongly indicate that private two-year colleges, like private Liberal Arts Colleges II, have difficult financial problems, especially if they are very small. Their comparatively high administrative costs in almost all size classes suggest that they probably spend relatively large sums on recruitment activities—almost certainly such expenditures are essential to their efforts to maintain their relatively small enrollments. On the other hand, they tend to economize on faculty salaries and on instructional expenditures

FTE students per FTE faculty‡		Mean full-time faculty salary†		Faculty salary expenditures† as a percentage of total educational and general expenditures§	
I	II	I	II	I	II
	7.8		$6,662		19
	12.2		7,087		22
9.5		$10,293		31	
	13.1		7,441		25
12.2	14.4	9,539	7,908	31	28
12.7	15.3	10,033	8,244	31	29
11.6	17.4	9,973	8,331	31	29
13.4	16.6	10,203	8,525	33	32
15.9	18.3	10,293	8,933	32	31
	19.4		9,718		30
13.1*		10,855*		27*	
12.8	14.6	10,046	7,976	31	28
106	437	106	437	106	437

generally. Clearly, also, their problems—as a group of institutions but not necessarily in individual cases—have become increasingly difficult since 1967–68, the year to which these data refer. As we have noted elsewhere,[7] the number of private two-year colleges has declined in the last few years, and their enrollments have been falling off.

Finally, our experiments with multivariate analysis have yielded some interesting results, on which we shall comment briefly here. In these experiments, instructional and departmental research ex-

[7] *New Students and New Places*, p. 22.

TABLE C-19
Number of fields
and FTE faculty
per field in
which a degree
is offered,
student-faculty
ratios, and
faculty salary
data in two-year
colleges, public
and private, by
FTE enrollment,
1967–68

FTE enrollment	Number of fields in which a degree is offered		Resident FTE faculty per field in which a degree is offered†	
	Public	Private	Public	Private
0–199	9	8	1	1
200–399	13	10	2	2
400–599	14	11	2	3
600–799	15	12	3	3
800–999	16	13	3	4
1,000–1,249	17	10	3	5
1,250–1,499	18	15	4	2
1,500–1,999	21	16*	4	4*
2,000–2,499	23	15*	5	9*
2,500–2,999	23		5	
3,000–3,999	26	13*	6	8*
4,000–4,999	28		4	
5,000–7,499	24		9	
7,500–19,999	29		16	
Mean	18	11	4	2
Number of institutions reporting	375	150	375	150

* Based on fewer than five cases.

† Includes all faculty ranks of instructor and above plus teaching assistants and other junior faculty.

‡ Includes all faculty ranks of instructor and above, but not teaching assistants and other junior faculty.

§ Educational and general expenditures minus organized (sponsored and other separately budgeted) research.

SOURCE: Adapted from U.S. Office of Education data (Higher Education General Information Survey) by Carnegie Commission staff.

penditures per student (using total enrollment rather than FTE enrollment) was the dependent variable; the independent variables were (1) total enrollment, (2) part-time enrollment as a percentage of total enrollment, (3) upper-division enrollment as a percentage of undergraduate enrollment; (4) freshman enrollment as a percentage of undergraduate enrollment; (5) graduate enrollment as a percentage of total enrollment; (6) teachers' certificates or B.A.'s in education as a percentage of total degrees granted; (7) science degrees as a percentage of total degrees granted; (8) nondegree-credit enroll-

FTE students per FTE faculty‡		Mean full-time faculty salary†		Faculty salary expenditures† as a percentage of total educational and general expenditures§	
Public	Private	Public	Private	Public	Private
15.2	8.5	$ 7,558	$4,404	41	13
14.4	14.3	7,977	6,757	39	23
18.6	17.2	8,025	6,985	39	29
18.9	19.7	8,258	7,004	37	27
20.8	20.5	8,266	6,948	36	21
20.9	26.6	8,119	7,901	38	31
19.4	39.7	8,446	7,310	38	26
23.9	24.0*	8,922	7,500*	41	26*
21.5	16.4*	9,447	7,435*	35	31*
24.9		9,491		38	
22.4	30.4*	9,828	6,524*	38	31*
35.0		9,700		35	
29.9		10,371		34	
27.0		10,761		33	
20.6	15.7	8,601	6,638	38	24
375	150	375	150	375	150

ment as a percentage of total enrollment; (9) mean faculty salary; (10) number of fields in which degrees were granted; (11) student-faculty ratio; (12) full professors as percentage of total faculty; (13) faculty members with Ph.D.'s as percentage of faculty members with master's or higher degrees, and (14) number of faculty members per field.

We present illustrative results only for public comprehensive universities and colleges, but similar results were obtained for other groups of institutions (Table C-20). The average adjusted instructional costs per student resulting from the econometric equations used in the multivariate analysis show a much more consistent and pronounced decline with increasing enrollment when fixed (overall) means for the independent variables were used in the equations than the unadjusted data show. A similarly consistent but less pronounced decline in instructional costs per student was obtained when fixed means were used for most independent variables, but means that varied by size class were used for (1) student-faculty ratios, (2) number of fields, and (3) number of faculty members per field. When variable means were used for all independent variables, the results were closer to the unadjusted costs by size class than on the basis of either of the first two methods.

TABLE C-20
Illustrative results of multivariate analysis — instructional and departmental research expenditures per student, by total enrollment, public comprehensive universities and colleges, 1967–68

		Adjusted data (derived from econometric equations)		
Total enrollment	*Unadjusted data*	*Fixed means**	*Variable means†*	*Fixed and variable means‡*
0–2,499	643	1,339	689	740
2,500–3,499	598	916	666	697
3,500–5,999	647	684	698	682
6,000–7,999	632	533	628	598
8,000–11,999	577	431	591	585
12,000 and over	585	311	541	481

* Fixed (overall) means were used for all independent variables.

† Means that varied by size class were used for all independent variables.

‡ Fixed (overall) means were used for most variables, but means that varied by size class were used for (1) student to faculty ratios, (2) number of fields, and (3) number of faculty members per field.

SOURCE: Adapted from U.S. Office of Education data (Higher Education General Information Survey) by Daryl Carlson of the Carnegie Commission staff.

An interesting by-product of this analysis is that a variable which was not included, and is not shown in Tables C-1 to C-19 — number of nonprofessional employees per student — showed a sharp and very persistent decline with increasing enrollment, from 0.82 in the smallest size class to 0.10 in the largest size class. This finding, along with the evidence that student-faculty ratios rise quite consistently with increasing enrollment in most groups of institutions, at least up to a certain point, indicates that institutions of higher education can generally make more effective use of their employees as they increase in size. The fact that overall economies in educational costs per FTE student with increasing size are not nearly so clearcut appears to result chiefly from the tendency for institutions —especially universities, comprehensive universities and colleges— to become more complex and to add relatively expensive fields of study as they grow in size. And, as we have seen, in some groups of institutions, faculty salaries tend to rise with increasing size— another factor working against economies of scale.

Appendix D: Excerpt from Statement on Faculty Workload of the American Association of University Professors

BACKGROUND EXPLANATION *A Statement on Faculty Workload, prepared by Committee C on Teaching, Research, and Publication, was published in the Summer 1968 Bulletin, at the direction of the Council of the Association. This statement incorporated revisions made in response to comments received from members, chapters, conferences, and other interested parties as a result of the publication of a draft statement on this subject in the Winter 1968, issue of the Bulletin.*

The Council approved the revised Statement on Faculty Workload at its October 1968, meeting. The Fifty-fifth Annual Meeting in 1969 voted its endorsement of the Statement, but with an amendment that called for revising the recommended teaching load from twelve and nine hours to nine and six.

While recognizing that many members of the profession prefer setting forth a nine- and six-hour standard, the Council expressed doubt that this standard could be realistically applied at the present time at two-year institutions and many private and public four-year colleges. It therefore referred the matter back to Committee C, with the suggestion that an attempt be made to reconcile the two recommendations. The new version of the Statement which follows, recommended by Committee C and approved by the Council at its October 1969, meeting, incorporates both a maximum and a preferred standard. The Fifty-sixth Annual Meeting will be asked to consider and to endorse this revised version of the Statement.

INTRODUCTION No single formula for an equitable faculty workload can be devised for all of American higher education. What is fair and works well in the community college may be inappropriate for the university,

NOTE: Reprinted from the *AAUP Bulletin*, Spring 1970.

and the arrangement thought necessary in the technical institute may be irrelevant in the liberal arts college.

This is not to say, however, that excessive or inequitably distributed workloads cannot be recognized as such. In response to the many appeals received in recent years, therefore, this Association wishes to set forth such guidelines as can be applied generally, regardless of the special circumstances of the institution concerned:

(1) A definition of maximum teaching loads for effective instruction at the undergraduate and graduate levels.

(2) A description of the procedures that should be followed in establishing, administering, and revising workload policies.

(3) An identification of the most common sources of inequity in the distribution of workloads.

MAXIMUM TEACHING LOADS In the American system of higher education, faculty "workloads" are usually described in hours per week of formal class meetings. As a measurement, this leaves much to be desired. It fails to consider other time-consuming institutional duties of the faculty member, and, even in terms of his teaching, it misrepresents the true situation. The teacher normally spends far less time in the classroom than in preparation, conferences, grading of papers and examinations, and supervision of remedial or advanced student work. Preparation, in particular, is of critical importance, and is probably the most unremitting of these demands: not only preparation for specific classes or conferences, but that more general preparation in the discipline, by keeping up with recent developments and strengthening his grasp on older materials, without which the faculty member will soon dwindle into ineffectiveness as scholar and teacher. Moreover, traditional workload formulations are at odds with significant current developments in education emphasizing independent study, the use of new materials and media, extracurricular and off-campus educational experiences, and interdisciplinary approaches to problems in contemporary society. Policies on workload at institutions practicing such approaches suggest the need for a more sophisticated discrimination and weighting of educational activities.

This Association has been in a position over the years to observe workload policies and faculty performance in a great variety of American colleges and universities, and in its considered judgment the following maximum workload limits are necessary for any institution of higher education seriously intending to achieve and sustain an adequately high level of faculty effectiveness in teaching and scholarship:

For undergraduate instruction, a teaching load of twelve hours per week, with no more than six separate course preparations during the academic year.

For instruction partly or entirely at the graduate level, a teaching load of nine hours per week.

This statement of maximum workload presumes a traditional academic year of not more than thirty-two weeks of classes. Moreover, it presumes no unusual additional expectations in terms of research, administration, counseling, or other institutional responsibilities. Finally, it presumes also that means can be devised within each institution for determining fair equivalents in workload for those faculty members whose activities do not fit the conventional classroom lecture or discussion pattern: for example, those who supervise laboratories or studios, offer tutorials, or assist beginning teachers.

Even with the reservations just made, however, it would be misleading to offer this statement of maximum loads without providing some guidelines for a preferable pattern. This Association has observed in recent years a steady reduction of teaching loads in American colleges and universities noted for the effectiveness of their faculties in teaching and scholarship to norms that can be stated as follows:

For undergraduate instruction, a teaching load of nine hours per week.

For instruction partly or entirely at the graduate level, a teaching load of six hours per week.

The Association has observed also that in the majority of these institutions further reductions have become quite usual for individuals assuming heavier than normal duties in counseling, program development, administration, research, and many other activities. In a smaller number, moreover, even lower teaching loads have been established generally, for all faculty members.

It must be recognized that achievement of nine- or six-hour teaching loads may not be possible at present for many institutions. The Association believes, nevertheless, that the nine- or six-hour loads achieved by our leading colleges and universities, in some instances many years ago, provide as reliable a guide as may be found for teaching loads in any institution intending to achieve and maintain excellence in faculty performance.

PROCEDURES The faculty should participate fully in the determination of work-load policy, both initially and in all subsequent reappraisals. Reappraisal at regular intervals is essential, in order that older patterns of faculty responsibility may be adjusted to changes in the institution's size, structure, academic programs, and facilities. Current policy and practices should be made known clearly to all faculty members, including those new to the institution each year.

The individual may have several quite different duties, some of which may be highly specialized, and the weight of these duties may vary strikingly at different times during the year. It is important, therefore, that individual workloads be determined by, or in consultation with, the department or other academic unit most familiar with the demands involved. Those responsible should be allowed a measure of latitude in making individual assignments, and care should be taken that all the individual's services to the institution are considered. (There follows a discussion of Common Sources of Inequity in The Distribution of Workloads.)

SOURCE: *AAUP Bulletin,* vol. 56, no. 1, March 1970, pp. 30–31.

References

1   Harris, S. E.: *Economics of Harvard*, McGraw-Hill Book Company, New York, 1970.

2   O'Neill, J.: *Resource Use in Higher Education: Trends in Output and Inputs, 1930 to 1967*, Carnegie Commission on Higher Education, Berkeley, Calif., 1971.

3   Baumol, William J., and William G. Bowen: *Performing Arts: The Economic Dilemma* © 1966 by The Twentieth Century Fund, New York.

4   Bowen, H. R.: "Financial Needs of the Campus," in *The Corporation and the Campus*, Academy of Political Science, 1970.

5   Cheit, E. F.: *The New Depression in Higher Education: A Study of Financial Conditions at 41 Colleges and Universities*, McGraw-Hill Book Company, New York, 1971.

6   Jellema, W. W.: *The Red and the Black: Special Preliminary Report on the Financial Status, Present and Projected, of Private Institutions of Higher Learning*, Association of American Colleges, Washington, D.C., n.d.

7   Jellema, W. W.: *Redder and Much Redder: A Follow-up Study to "The Red and the Black,"* Association of American Colleges, Washington, D.C., 1971.

8   *Chronicle of Higher Education*, April 27, 1970.

9   *Chronicle of Higher Education*, April 5, 1971.

10 Smith, V. B.: "More for Less: Higher Education's New Priority," in American Council on Education, *Universal Higher Education: Costs and Benefits*, Washington, D.C., 1971.

11 U.S. Office of Education: *Projections of Educational Statistics to 1979-80: 1970 Edition*, Washington, D.C., 1971.

12 *The Wall Street Journal*, December 27, 1971.

13 Cartter, A. M.: *An Assessment of Quality in Graduate Instruction*, American Council on Education, Washington, D.C., 1966.

14 Roose, K. D., and C. J. Andersen: *A Rating of Graduate Programs,* American Council on Education, Washington, D.C., 1970.

15 Williams College: *Memorandum of the Committee on Coordinate Education and Related Questions to the Faculty,* Williamstown, Mass., May 27, 1969.

16 Systems Research Group, University of Toronto: *Cost and Benefit Study of Post-Secondary Education in the Province of Ontario: School Year 1968–69,* Phase I, Toronto, 1970.

17 National Science Board and National Science Foundation: *Graduate Education: Parameters for Public Policy,* Washington, D.C., 1969.

18 Enthoven, A. C.: "Measures of the Outputs of Higher Education: Some Practical Suggestions for Their Development and Use," in B. Lawrence, G. Weathersby, and V. Patterson (eds.); *The Outputs of Higher Education: Their Identification, Measurement, and Evaluation,* Western Interstate Commission for Higher Education, Boulder, Colo., July 1970.

19 McKinsey & Company, Inc.: *The Twelve College Cost-Quality Study,* Washington, D.C., 1972.

20 *The Wall Street Journal,* July 15, 1971.

21 *Chronicle of Higher Education,* May 3, 1971.

22 *San Francisco Chronicle,* January 27, 1971.

23 *Chronicle of Higher Education,* July 5, 1971.

24 *Appleton, Wisconsin Post Crescent,* May 1, 1971.

25 *Deseret News,* Salt Lake City, Utah, November 19, 1971.

26 *St. Louis Globe-Democrat,* November 18, 1971.

27 *St. Louis Post Dispatch,* December 4, 1971.

28 *Columbia, Missouri Tribune,* November 21, 1971.

29 *The Capitol Times,* Madison, Wis., December 8, 1971.

30 Colgate University, institutional publication, November 1971.

31 Princeton University: *A Report to the Commission on the Future of the College from Marvin Bressler for Discussion by the Princeton University Community,* November 1971.

32 *Chronicle of Higher Education,* April 17. 1972.

33 *Chronicle of Higher Education,* February 29, 1972.

34 *Chronicle of Higher Education,* May 10, 1971.

35 *Chronicle of Higher Education,* June 7, 1971.

36 *Chronicle of Higher Education,* April 26, 1971.

37 *Chronicle of Higher Education,* June 7, 1971.

38 **U.S. Bureau of the Census:** "School Enrollment: October 1970," *Current Population Reports,* series P-20, no. 222, Washington, D.C., 1971.

39 *Chronicle of Higher Education,* March 27, 1972.

40 *New York Times,* November 14, 1971.

41 *Chronicle of Higher Education,* January 3, 1972.

42 **The Council of Graduate Schools in the United States:** *Supplemental Statement on the Doctor of Arts Degree, 1972,* Washington, D.C., December 1971.

43 **Harris, S. E.:** *A Statistical Portrait of Higher Education,* McGraw-Hill Book Company, New York, 1972.

44 **Astin, A.:** *College Dropouts: A National Profile,* American Council on Education, Washington, D.C., 1972.

45 **U.S. Office of Education:** *Retention and Withdrawal of College Students,* Washington, D.C., 1957.

46 **Radner, R.:** "Faculty-Student Ratios in U.S. Higher Education," to be published in a volume of conference papers, *Education as an Industry,* by the National Bureau of Economic Research.

47 **Jenny, H. H., and G. R. Wynn:** *The Golden Years: A Study of Income and Expenditure Growth and Distribution of 48 Private Four-year Liberal Arts Colleges, 1960–1968,* The College of Wooster, Wooster, Ohio, 1970.

48 Analyses by the Carnegie Commission staff based on HEGIS data.

49 **Bowen, W. G.:** *The Economics of the Major Private Universities,* Carnegie Commission on Higher Education, Berkeley, Calif., 1968.

50 **State of California, Coordinating Council for Higher Education:** *Higher Cost Programs in California Public Higher Education,* Council Report 71-3, Sacramento, 1971.

51 **Ruml, B., with D. H. Morrison:** *Memo to a College Trustee: A Report on Financial and Structural Problems of the Liberal Arts College,* McGraw-Hill Book Company, New York, 1959.

52 **Bowen, H. R., and G. K. Douglass:** *Efficiency in Liberal Education: A Study of Comparative Instructional Costs for Different Ways of Organizing Teaching-Learning in a Liberal Arts College,* McGraw-Hill Book Company, New York, 1971.

53 *Business Week,* October 30, 1971.

54 **National Center for Higher Education Management Systems at WICHE:** *Faculty Activity Analysis: Overview and Major Issues,* Technical Report No. 24, Boulder, Colo., 1971.

55 New York University: *Progress Report,* Commission on the Effective Use of Resources, September 1970.

56 *Chronicle of Higher Education,* August 3, 1970.

57 *Chronicle of Higher Education,* December 13, 1971.

58 Princeton University: *Report of the Priorities Committee to the President: Recommendations Concerning the Budget for Fiscal Year 1971–72,* January 20, 1971.

59 Balderston, F. E.: "Varieties of Financial Crisis," in American Council on Education, *Universal Higher Education: Costs and Benefits,* Washington, D.C., 1971.

60 U.S. Office of Education: *Digest of Educational Statistics, 1970,* Washington, D.C., 1970.

61 *Survey of Current Business, seriatim.*

62 Garbarino, J. S.: "Creeping Unionism and the Faculty Labor Market," to be included in *Higher Education and the Labor Market,* a volume of essays to be published by McGraw-Hill Book Company for the Carnegie Commission on Higher Education.

63 Peterson, R. E.: *American College and University Enrollment Trends in 1971,* Carnegie Commission on Higher Education, Berkeley, Calif., 1972.

64 Freeman, R. B.: *The Market for College Trained Manpower: A Study of the Economics of Career Choice,* Harvard University Press, Cambridge, Mass., 1971.

65 Freeman, R. B.: *The Science Manpower Market in the 1970s,* unpublished paper, University of Chicago, 1971.

66 National Science Foundation: *Summary of Conclusions: 1969 and 1980 Science and Engineering Doctorate Supply and Utilization,* NSF 71-20, Washington, D.C., 1971.

67 U.S. Bureau of Labor Statistics: *The U.S. Economy in 1980: A Summary of BLS Projections,* Bulletin 1673, Washington, D.C., 1971.

68 *Chronicle of Higher Education,* December 6, 1971.

69 *Memoranda of Provost John T. Wilson to the Faculty,* The University of Chicago, July 31, 1970, and September 7, 1971.

70 Mayhew, L. B.: *Graduate and Professional Education, 1980: A Survey of Institutional Plans,* McGraw-Hill Book Company, New York, 1970.

71 Princeton University: *Report of the Priorities Committee to the President, Recommendations Concerning the Budget for Fiscal Year 1972–73,* January 31, 1972.

72 *The Tech,* Massachusetts Institute of Technology, Cambridge, Mass., November 12, 1971.

73 Information supplied by Chancellor Allan M. Cartter, New York University.

74 *New York Times,* December 8, 1971.

75 *Campus Report Supplement,* Stanford University, Stanford, Calif., April 17, 1970.

76 *Campus Report Supplement,* Stanford University, Stanford, Calif., April 22, 1971.

77 **Office of the President, University of California:** *Budget for Current Operations, 1971–72,* Berkeley, Calif., September 18, 1970.

78 Information supplied by Professor Paul V. Grambsch, School of Management, University of Minnesota.

79 **Hudgins, G., and I. Phillips:** *A Financial Profile of the Nation's State Universities and Land-Grant Colleges,* National Association of State Universities and Land-Grant Colleges, 1971.

80 *The University of Washington Report,* May 31, 1971.

81 *The Chronicle of Higher Education,* May 24, 1971.

82 **Harvard University, The University Committee on Governance:** *Harvard and Money: A Memorandum on Issues and Choices,* Cambridge, Mass., 1970.

83 *Report of the Subcommittee on the Status of Academic Women on the Berkeley Campus,* Academic Senate, Berkeley Division, University of California, May 19, 1970.

84 *Chronicle of Higher Education,* December 13, 1971.

85 **Teachers Insurance and Annuity Association—College Retirement Equities Fund:** *Annual Report,* 1968.

86 Information supplied by Provost John T. Wilson, University of Chicago.

87 Information supplied by William Slater, vice president, Teachers Insurance and Annuity Association.

88 **Gallaway, L. E.:** *The Retirement Decision: An Exploratory Essay,* U.S. Social Security Administration, Research Report No. 9, Washington, D.C., 1965.

89 **Pechman, J. A., H. J. Aaron, and M. K. Taussig:** *Social Security: Perspectives for Reform,* The Brookings Institution, Washington, D.C., 1968.

90 **Gordon, M. S.:** "Income Security Programs and the Propensity to Retire," in R. H. Williams, C. Tibbitts, and W. Donahue (eds.), *Processes of Aging,* Prentice-Hall, Inc., Atherton Press, New York, 1963.

91 *Chronicle of Higher Education,* October 18, 1971.

92 **Hayward, S.:** "The Beloit Plan," *Liberal Education,* vol. 50, pp. 1–14, October 1964.

93 **Beloit College:** *The Beloit Plan,* Beloit, Wis., 1971.

94 Miscellaneous memoranda provided by Beloit College.

95 Dochterman, C. L.: "The California Experiment: A Case Study," *Compact,* vol. 4, pp. 29–30, December 1970.

96 California State Department of Education: *A Master Plan for Higher Education in California: 1960–1975,* Sacramento, 1960.

97 Smith, D.: "Optimal Class Scheduling," *College and University,* vol. 44, pp. 383–401, Summer 1969.

98 State of Illinois Board of Higher Education: *Comprehensive Study of Space Planning Standards: Preliminary Report to Participating Institutions,* Springfield, 1971.

99 *San Francisco Chronicle,* March 9, 1972.

100 Association of Independent Colleges and Universities of Ohio: *Toward an Effective Utilization of Independent Colleges and Universities by the State of Ohio,* Columbus, Ohio, 1971.

101 *New York Times,* October 3, 1971.

102 Academy for Educational Development, Management Division: *A Guide to Professional Development Opportunities for College and University Administrators, January–December 1972,* New York, 1971.

103 American Academy of Arts and Sciences: *A First Report: The Assembly on University Goals and Governance,* Cambridge, Mass., 1971.

104 National Education Association: *Salaries Paid and Salary Practices in Universities, Colleges and Junior Colleges, 1959–60,* Washington, D.C., 1960.

105 National Education Association: *Salaries in Higher Education, 1969–70.* Washington, D.C., 1970.

106 Cornell University: *Study of Rising Costs at Ten Universities,* Ithaca, N.Y., 1967.

107 Information supplied by Vice President John Wynne, Massachusetts Institute of Technology.

108 Fein, R., and G. L. Weber: *Financing Medical Education: An Analysis of Alternative Policies and Mechanisms,* McGraw-Hill Book Company, New York, 1971.

109 U.S. Department of Health, Education and Welfare: *Financial Distress Study Report,* December 1971.

110 *New York Times,* March 10, 1971.

111 "State Appropriations to Teaching Hospitals," *Journal of Medical Education,* vol. 45, pp. 260–261, April 1970.

112 Carnegie Commission on Higher Education: *Higher Education and the Nation's Health: Policies for Medical and Dental Education,* McGraw-Hill Book Company, New York, 1970.

113 *New York Times,* March 14, 1972.

114 Binning, D. W.: "1969–1970 College Operating Practices," *College and University Business,* vol. 47, pp. 47–62, November 1969.

115 *Harvard Today,* March 1972.

116 Cary, W. L., and C. B. Bright: *The Law and Lore of Endowment Funds: Report to the Ford Foundation,* New York, 1969.

117 Ford Foundation Advisory Committee on Endowment Management: *Managing Educational Endowments,* The Ford Foundation, New York, 1969.

118 Meyerson, M.: "In Pursuit of Sharpened Goals," *Pennsylvania Gazette,* February 1972, pp. 9–15.

119 Dressel, P. L., and Associates: *Institutional Research in the University,* Jossey-Bass, Inc., San Francisco, 1971.

120 Maynard, J.: *Some Microeconomics of Higher Education: Economies of Scale,* University of Nebraska Press, Lincoln, 1971.